Somebody's
Child

Somebody's

The story of a man who found hope – and took it back to the streets

Child

John Robinson
with Jan Greenough

MONARCH
BOOKS

Oxford, UK & Grand Rapids, Michigan, USA

First published in the UK in 2007 by Monarch Books
(a publishing imprint of Lion Hudson plc),
Mayfield House, 256 Banbury Road, Oxford, OX2 7DH.
Tel: +44 (0) 1865 302750   Fax: +44 (0) 1865 302757
Email: monarch@lionhudson.com
www.lionhudson.com

ISBN: 978-1-85424-852-7 (UK)
ISBN: 978-0-8254-6149-1 (USA)

Distributed by:
UK: Marston Book Services Ltd, PO Box 269,
Abingdon, Oxon OX14 4YN;
USA: Kregel Publications, PO Box 2607,
Grand Rapids, Michigan 49501.

The text paper used in this book has been made from wood inde-
pendently certified as having come from sustainable forests.

British Library Cataloguing Data
A catalogue record for this book is available
from the British Library.

CONTENTS

DEDICATION

To Gillian and my precious girls, Natalie and Leah:
I love you so much and pray that you will always
know you are not alone.

To everyone who feels alone in the world, as I did,
that you would know that you are somebody's child.

ACKNOWLEDGMENTS

Thank you to Gillian: not only am I grateful to have you in my life, but truly blessed to have such a good friend who has been with me through all the ups and downs. Thanks also to Gillian's family, for all your love and support.

I am also grateful to Jan Greenough: without your constant encouragement and phone calls we would not have been able to finish the book.

To those involved in the bus ministry who have given so much: without you we couldn't have reached so many young people for God.

Lastly, to everyone who has been working prayerfully and financially behind the scenes: you are a great support and strength. There are so many of you I couldn't begin to thank you all – you know who you are. God bless you.

John Robinson

FOREWORDS

The Eden Bus Ministry that John Robinson heads up works out of an office here at The Message Trust. A few days ago I was wandering through the office with another member of the team when I noticed a pile of books that John had been sent by his publisher. It was the latest batch of translations of John's life story, *Nobody's Child*, in Hungarian, Dutch, Korean and German. I said to my colleague, 'Isn't God amazing, that he can take someone like John, who was utterly broken, had no hope and was sleeping in shop doorways, and use them to bless the world?'

I'm sure that with the release of *Somebody's Child* even more people will be touched and inspired by John's ongoing journey. But I also know that what John longs for most of all is that through this important book, the most marginalized and hurting individuals will be given hope, and that their lives can also be turned round and set on a course that takes them, as Psalm 40 so poetically puts it, 'out of the slimy pit, out of the mud and mire, and sets their feet on a rock...so that many will see and fear and put their trust in the Lord'.

Every week here at The Message we gather all the

different teams working on the estates, in the schools and in the prisons across Greater Manchester for a time of prayer and encouragement. During these times John will invariably have a testimony to share with us about some tough young person who has encountered Jesus through the Bus Ministry. As he shares their difficult lives and the joy of salvation, we all love it and wait for John to say what has become his catchphrase – 'It brings a tear to your eye!' At this point a great cheer goes round the room.

Isn't it great that John's tears have gone from tears of brokenness and rejection to tears of joy over the salvation of needy young people just like him, and don't you just love the God who specializes in doing that with people, whether it be in South Korea, Holland, Thailand, Hungary, Germany or on the streets of Manchester?

Andy Hawthorne
Chief Executive, The Message Trust

John Robinson displays many gifts and talents whilst engaged in his varied ministries, including the Eden Bus, where he works with local young people in some of the most difficult areas of Greater Manchester. He has an amazing ability to share his personal experiences of hope and a changed life with the young people, who often feel hopeless and are sometimes on the edge of criminality. This is so refreshing in a world where others often spend hours agonizing over the best way to engage with young people – John just gets on and does it. *Somebody's Child* embodies this hope.

Alison Fletcher
Police Superintendent in Stockport
and previously in Salford

Chapter 1

When *Nobody's Child* **was published,** I was amazed at the response. People bought that book and read it and lent it to their friends, and lots of them wrote to me and emailed me, telling me their own stories. You'll find some of them in this book, because God is still working in my life and in theirs, and what he does is always amazing. *Somebody's Child* tells the story of what has been happening since then. For those who haven't read *Nobody's Child*, this chapter fills in a bit of the background.

I never knew anything about my family when I was young. I grew up in care, and the social workers were careful not to give me much information. It was only when I was an adult, and discovered that the law allowed me to see my own records, that I was able to find out anything about my background. The records stated that neither of my parents wanted me: my father was in prison and my mother, an alcoholic, was living on benefits. When she went out drinking, she left the children locked in the house. By the time I was taken into care at five months old, I was already suffering from neglect.

Apparently I lived in several foster homes over the years, but every placement failed. I don't remember much about that: I only have vague memories of a couple of homes, and they aren't happy ones. In one of them I was beaten with a broom-handle, and in another I was forced to strip and smacked with a slipper. In one I slept in a bare attic divided into four cubicles, unable to play with the other three children locked in with me; when I wet the bed they made me eat mustard sandwiches, which made me sick. One day, after breakfast, my foster mother stripped me naked and put me in the cellar, and left me there all day in the dark and cold while she went to work.

Eventually, when I was about nine years old, I was sent to a Barnardo's home in Tadcaster, a few miles outside York. That home was the closest I ever got to family life, and the staff tried hard to give us the kind of love, security and guidance that children need. I was happy there. My only real sadness was that no one in my family had ever tried to make contact with me. Other kids received presents and cards on their birthdays; I only ever had a card from the staff. Every year, at Christmas and birthdays, that rejection by my family was rubbed in, until it seemed to shape my whole life. Even among the other children in care, I stood out as the boy nobody wanted.

As I grew up I realized that being a Barnardo's boy was always going to mark me out. At secondary school there was a stigma attached to being in care, and girls didn't want to go out with me. Later on I got lazy about studying and my school-work began to suffer. There didn't seem to be any point in trying to prepare for the future when no one took any interest in me. I wanted so much to belong to a group and have friends of my own, and I started hanging around with some older lads in the town.

We used to climb over a fence at the back of the Yorkshire breweries and collect reject beer cans with dents in them, and we had a great time drinking and being rowdy. As we got older we got cocky, off-loading a crate here and there. We were cautioned a few times by the police, but no one took it too seriously. Then one night we lifted some beer and went out to a nearby barn to drink it. While we were messing around a candle fell over into a bale of straw, and to our horror the whole barn went up in flames. The police arrived, and I was charged with arson. Even though I told everyone it was an accident, I was found guilty and sentenced to six weeks in a detention centre.

The detention centre was horrible: I was only fourteen, and most of the time I was terrified. I got beaten up a lot and started wetting the bed again, which made the bullying worse. When I was released I was glad to get back home to Barnardo's, and I vowed that I was never going to get into trouble again. Then the blow fell: as soon as I turned sixteen I would have to leave – my place was needed for a younger child.

Leaving Barnardo's seemed like the end of the world. I left school at the same time – what was the point of taking exams when I already had a criminal record? No one would ever give me a job. Emotionally I was still very immature, and I had no idea how to take care of myself. Once again I started hanging out with the wrong lads, drinking in the pub and trying to look big. They were all involved in crime – shoplifting and stealing cars – and I went along with it. It felt like adventure, and I thought it was exciting. We did a couple of burglaries of commercial premises – we never did houses, but we reckoned the shops could afford to lose a bit, and anyway the insurance companies would pay.

I lived in a squat with a group of my mates, and it was horrible – filthy and smelling of vomit and urine. Most of the people there were on drugs, and you could get hold of anything if you wanted it. I tried LSD once but it gave me terrible nightmares, so I kept off it. In spite of acting big, I was often afraid – fights could break out over nothing. I felt I needed to be in control if I was going to take care of myself.

I was always wary and on edge, because you never knew what would happen next. Sometimes it was a raid by another gang, looking for a fight. Sometimes it was a raid by the police, looking for drugs or stolen goods. We always seemed to be running away from something. I carried a Bowie knife – a dagger with a blade about a foot long – and I set about establishing a reputation for toughness, getting tattoos and acting big. Only I knew that inside I wasn't tough at all. I was living a hard, fast, dangerous life, and sometimes I was sure I would die from it: one fight too many, picked with the wrong person, and that would be it. I was mixing with a criminal crowd, and they were all in and out of prison all the time. They were violent, too. I lost count of the number of times I was admitted to hospital with stab wounds, bruises or cuts that needed stitches. I've got some dramatic scars. Every time I tried to leave the gang I was beaten up. It was a terrible life but I didn't know how to get out, and I didn't know anyone outside it. I was on my own – what choice did I have?

I ended up in prison for burglary – and that was so awful that I tried to commit suicide. When I came out after eighteen months I slipped back into my old ways, mainly because there was no support to help me find a job or anywhere to live, and after a while I was arrested yet again. I could see that I was sliding down the slope towards becoming one of the old lags I'd met in jail – men who had drifted in and out of prison all their lives.

Then I got a lucky break from a compassionate judge who offered me one more chance: a Conditional Discharge, which meant that I was released to a bail hostel. This time I wasn't going to blow it. I got a job, I kept the rules, and I started putting my life back together. It nearly worked, too. I got a good job in a factory. I met a girl and got married, and even bought a house. I had a wife and good friends, and I thought I really had it made. Then, just like before, everything fell apart.

One night when I was working the late shift I realized I'd left my sandwiches at home and went back for them. I found my wife at home with my best friend, at two o'clock in the morning. I felt sure that they were having an affair. I couldn't cope with the shock, so I just walked out and left everything, even my job. I felt the betrayal more keenly, I think, because I had always felt so alone. I'd dreamt all my life of having a family of my own, and now it had all been snatched away again. I went back on the streets, living rough and getting into fights, nearly starving and not caring what happened to me. One doctor who stitched up my cuts was so concerned about my depressed state of mind that he sent me to a mental hospital for a while, but when I came out I was still living the same hopeless, lonely life as before. Nobody cared about me.

I slept on the street if I couldn't find a squat or a mate with a spare floor; sometimes I managed to get a place in a hostel. Some of those hostels were truly awful places, with big gates and barbed wire round the walls – more to keep the local vandals out than to keep the residents in. Often they were used as 'resettlement centres' for recovering drug addicts and alcoholics, as well as hostels for the homeless, and lots of the men were in a bad way. Some drank meths when they couldn't get hold of anything else, and several were incontinent and always vomiting. No matter how much disinfectant was used, the place always smelt bad. I could see why so many of the residents found it hard to give up the habits that were destroying them – it was their only way of escape from the awful reality of their lives.

We were all unemployed. One of our problems was that the hostels had a really bad reputation, so even when there were jobs available, no one would take us on when they knew where we were living. For a while I went round with a sack, collecting old cans and using a magnet to find out if they were aluminium – you could make a bit of money that way. Spending the day walking round searching the ground for other people's rubbish made me think, 'I'm just a piece of rubbish myself.' I felt so alone.

I met all sorts of people in those hostels – some of

them were 'men of the road', who walked from town to town, staying in hostels in the winter months and sleeping outside when it was warmer. Many of them weren't so bad, and they still had some self-esteem and a kind of dignity. Others were deeply depressed and in despair, men who would drink or smoke or inject almost anything to achieve oblivion. One man didn't do drugs or alcohol but he was always cutting himself: his emotional state was so bad that self-harming was the only way he could express his pain.

I never wanted to do that, but I could understand him. When no one cares about you, you don't care about yourself. There had been times in my life when I didn't care whether I lived or died. I thought I'd escaped from that sort of despair once, and yet here I was again at the bottom of the pile. What hope was there now that anyone would ever take an interest in me?

It was while I was living like this, drifting from hostel to hostel, that God reached out and put his hand on me. I'd been taken to church as a child, but I thought religion was pretty boring, really, so when I came across some Christians singing in the street I wasn't interested. But one of them came over and started talking to me, and invited me to a meeting in the Town Hall. I don't know why I went – except that they all looked so happy, and the man, Tony, seemed genuinely interested in me. 'Jesus loves you,' he said, and somehow it didn't sound stupid when he said it. All I'd ever wanted was someone to love me and make me feel I was a real person, and now his words re-awakened this terrible longing in me.

I went to the meeting and I met God – that's the only way I can explain it. I suddenly understood, without a doubt, that although nobody on this earth seemed to care about me, God did. Even though I had been a criminal and a fighter and I'd never lived the way God wanted me to, he didn't blame me. Jesus had taken all the blame for me, and I could make a fresh start if I really wanted to. All I had to do was accept his love.

There were tears pouring down my face. I felt as if God was saying, 'John, you're special to me.' It was a fantastic feeling. I thought, 'I've been stabbed and beaten and people have robbed things off me, but no one can take God away from me.'

That was the moment when I became a Christian. I put my life in God's hands, without any idea where it might lead me. At that time, just knowing God's love was enough. I didn't have any expectations about how it was going to change my life.

In fact, God was leading me out of the hopeless pit my life had become, to a place where I could be useful for him, but it wasn't an easy journey. I'd never lived in a real home, and I didn't know how to trust people. I needed to gain some self-esteem, to learn how to be responsible and considerate, and how to take part in the give and take of family life. God lined up some wonderful Christians to play a part in helping me. Tony and his wife Sylvia in Sittingbourne, the Network Team in Deptford, Joey and Bridie the travellers, Julie and Ian on the Isle of Wight, and the community at Lee Abbey all took me in, one after another, and led me along the road to a life where I mattered.

I grew as a Christian, studying the Bible and taking courses in discipleship with the Ichthus Christian Fellowship. I got involved in soup runs, serving the homeless in the East End of London – it wasn't so long since I'd been scavenging in bins myself. For the first time in years there was a purpose to my life. I learned about forgiveness, and went through the pain and emotional healing of learning to forgive all the people who had hurt me.

I stayed with Tony and Sylvia for about a year, and living in their home taught me a lot. I'll never forget them because their love and care gradually chipped away some of my rough edges and taught me how to live with other people as a family. It couldn't have been easy for them, because when they took me in I was in a terrible state – physically unwell and emotionally exhausted. I tested them out a bit, because I couldn't believe that they could really love me. One night I went out and got really drunk and was sick on the floor. All they said was, 'We still love you, John, but you've got to clean up the mess yourself.' They showed me that I had to take responsibility for my actions, and helped me to grow as a person. They really lived out the love of God, and they helped me to understand God's unconditional love for us.

It sounds so easy to say that God changed my life, but it wasn't quick and it wasn't simple. Just as my body was marked by the life I'd led – covered in tattoos as well as scars from the beatings and stabbings – so my mind and my emotions were scarred by the loneliness, the rejections, the years of hoping and longing for love. I was used to pushing people away and putting up barriers because I couldn't face getting hurt all over again. Sometimes I found it difficult when we talked in the study group about drugs, alcohol, divorce, and all the other things that damage people's lives, because I was still sensitive about lots of things. Sometimes my tears were very near the surface as I spoke about the effect those things had had on my own life, but I felt safe and protected with my new friends around me and praying with me. Those Christians in the Fellowship became the brothers and sisters I'd never had, and I found a burning passion to share the love of Jesus with other people. I knew it could transform lives.

Lee Abbey in particular was a great place to grow as a Christian, because when you live in a community you can't hide your feelings or pretend anything. I learned self-discipline (for example, getting up on time and preparing properly when it was my turn to lead a prayer meeting), tolerance and love. That was when God gave me an even greater gift, the one thing I had always longed for – someone who was special to me and who loved me for myself.

I met Gillian when she was staying at Lee Abbey for a couple of months as a 'working guest' – someone who lives and works alongside the community but isn't a permanent part of it. We used to go for long walks on the hills and beach, and as we got to know each other, I began to realize that this was more than just a friendship. I was afraid to ask her out – I told her that I couldn't do that unless she promised it would be serious. I was terrified of being hurt and let down yet again if I let myself love someone, but deep down we both knew that the feelings we had for each other were very special.

Something we had in common was a deep sense of vocation. Gillian had known from the age of fourteen that God wanted her to be ordained as a minister, but at that time her paster didn't agree with women's ministry. By the time she went back home to Southampton we knew we wanted to get married.

At last I knew it was time to move on again, to take up my responsibilities in the real world. I'd learned a lot, but most of all I knew with absolute certainty that Jesus would walk with me every day and be my constant companion. That gave me the courage to start the next phase of my life. I moved to Southampton and took a job as a care worker in a special school, and helped with the youth programme in the church where Gillian worked. We had a wonderful wedding and settled down to married life, doing our best to serve God in the work he had given us.

It was while we were in Southampton that I first got the idea for a bus ministry. I'd done some research for the local churches into why young people didn't go to church, and I knew they thought the church was irrelevant to them. I wanted to take the gospel out to the streets where they were hanging out with their mates, and I hit on the idea of getting a camper van which I could drive round the estates, offering them a place to sit and talk and have a hot drink. We got funding from the Bishop of Winchester, I collected a group of helpers, and soon the Streetwise project was up and running.

The van was popular with the kids. As they began

to trust us, they started to ask why we put so much effort into helping them, and we were able to tell them about Jesus. A number of them became Christians.

Meanwhile, Gillian still felt a strong calling to be ordained, and after a great deal of prayer she applied and was accepted at theological college in Bristol. We passed on the care of the Streetwise work to a colleague, and moved house. I took a job as a youth and children's worker while Gillian went to college. Leah, our first child, was born halfway through the course, and Gillian used to study with her books on top of the table and one foot rocking the baby underneath! I was studying, too, for a higher diploma in Youth and Community Work. I knew that I had to be properly qualified if I was going to continue doing this work that meant so much to me. It was a struggle. Several times I threw an essay into the fire in disgust because my dyslexia made writing so hard for me. I was over the moon when I got my diploma: ordinary John Robinson, brought up in care and knocked about on the streets, had achieved something special!

We went back to Southampton, where the Bishop had plans for us: a church where we could work together, where Gillian could exercise her gifts for ministry and I could run the youth work. Gillian worked as a curate in the church and I got out on the streets again, meeting young people, doing school visits, and setting up a new Streetwise project, on the same lines as the first one.

Life wasn't all plain sailing. Gillian had had a grumbling appendix for some time, and eventually, when the pain got very bad, she was taken into hospital for investigations. She was on the emergency surgery list for twenty-four hours, but there wasn't a slot for her, and I took Leah home because we didn't want her to see her mummy in such distress. I was at home, looking after Leah, when the appendix burst and the emergency operation was finally performed. There were complications – one lung collapsed and she developed a blood infection – and she became very seriously ill. For a while we didn't know if she would live or die, and I was desperate. Was I going to lose her? I was filled with such fear that my precious family might be snatched away from me again. Still, I held on to the fact that God was in charge. Whatever happened, he wouldn't desert me. I kept praying, and gradually Gillian pulled through.

When our second daughter Natalie was born, we had to juggle two children and two part-time jobs between us. Life was certainly complicated and challenging, but we knew we were doing God's will, and neither of us was afraid of hard work. We were happy and busy and looking forward to the future, but we had no idea what God was planning for us next.

Chapter 2

CATCHING THE VISION

By 1999 my life was different from anything I'd ever known. I had my own family, with two little girls who were mine, and so precious to me. I had a lovely wife who had her own calling and a strong relationship with God. I had my work with young people. And most of all, I had Jesus. This was something that had changed my life, but getting used to a different way of thinking was still a challenge. For as long as I could remember, I had lived with rejection as part of who I was. It was all I had ever known, and learning to live without it, and learning to trust God instead, was like taking the first steps on a journey – one I'm still making.

I had been a nobody all my life, nobody's child, and a person that nobody cared about. I knew now that I was somebody to God. That was clear in my mind from the moment I became a Christian – but I was still learning that I was a family man, cared for by my family, and I had to understand what that meant. For instance, if I was having a bad day I would go off on my own for the whole afternoon, just driving around or going for a long walk, and switch off my phone so no one could get in touch. It never occurred to me that Gillian might worry about me. I'd never had to consider anyone else's feelings like that. Nowadays I've learned that lesson, and I stay in touch.

One problem was that I was so terrified of being rejected that I used to get in first – I used to push people away before they rejected me. Gillian found that hard when we were first married, because she didn't understand what I was doing. Fortunately God understands what we need, and at that point he brought our friend Trish into Gillian's life to be a friend to her. Trish had lived with me in the community at Lee Abbey, so she knew me well. She understood the hurt I had been through and the ways I tended to deal with it, so she was able to pray with Gillian about it.

Getting upset like that was something that used to happen if we had even the smallest argument, because whenever I made a mistake I was always afraid that I'd blown it – I used to think that I was about to lose everything all over again. I had to learn that married couples have their disagreements, and that there are ways of talking about things and sorting them out, and making up after a row.

We had a lot of talking to do around that period, because Gillian's time as a curate was coming to an end. We always knew that we would be moving on from Southampton eventually, because ministers in the Anglican Church only serve as a curate for a maximum of four years. Gillian had spent three years in her first church; then in the fourth year she was moved to another parish within the team ministry, where she was curate-in-charge. That meant it was rather like being the vicar for that church, but with the team rector overseeing the whole team. It was a good dry run for her first post as a vicar, as she was free to work alone, but with the support of the team ministry behind her.

She enjoyed working there. It was a small, beautiful church with a friendly congregation, and plenty of opportunities to work with young families in particular. Preparing and leading three services on a Sunday as well as all the rest of the tasks involved in church ministry meant that it was hard work but very rewarding, and the church was growing. Towards the end of that year, as we were both praying about where God would lead us next, a friend in the church took Gillian aside.

'Whose job will you follow when you move on,' she said, 'yours or John's? You won't be able to get a job together.'

'Both,' said Gillian. She had it set in her mind that God would show us where to go, and that he would give us both work in the same place, however unlikely it sounded. The world was open to us and we would go wherever he wanted us. We tried not to be too anxious, just to trust God and keep praying. One day Gillian was praying while she did the ironing and she said to God, 'Lord, I'm tired of all this uncertainty. I really want to know, now, where we'll be going.' A few minutes later the phone rang. It was David Gillett, who had been the Principal of her theological college and was now the Bishop of Bolton. He said to her, 'How do you fancy coming up to work in this diocese?'

'I don't mind,' said Gillian. 'I'll go wherever God wants.'

'Well, a couple of parishes here have vacancies. What about coming and having a look?'

She travelled up alone to look around, while I stayed and looked after the children. She came home full of enthusiasm.

I had been looking around for my next step too. The week before, I had taken a group of our young people from Southampton to camp at Soul Survivor at Shepton Mallet. It's a Christian festival which offers worship, teaching and music in a style that young people can relate to. The kids loved it because it spoke to them in their own language, and they were amazed to see so many Christians in one place, camping in the grounds, listening to the music, studying the Bible and praising God together. They liked the bands, too, especially The World Wide Message Tribe. They thought it was really cool to see hundreds of young people jumping up and down to 'Jumping in the House of God'.

I was just as excited as they were. I could see that The Tribe were getting over their message about God in a way that our kids could understand. Then a guy got up and started talking about how we could live our lives for God, and I thought he was really good, too. It was Andy Hawthorne, who headed the band and led The Message Trust.

After their set I went back and found Andy. I explained who I was, and about my Bus Ministry in Southampton. 'It's all about getting out and meeting young people on the street, and talking in language they understand,' I said. 'Just like The Tribe. Would you be willing to come and play for us in Southampton?'

'OK,' said Andy, 'if you'll do something in return. I think you might be the man we need to come and head up our Bus Ministry in Manchester. Will you think about it?'

I was pretty surprised, but I said I would. His talk had been inspiring. His theme was 'no more hit and run' – the sort of evangelism where people visit an area to preach the gospel, but then leave and go back to their own (more comfortable) surroundings. He talked about not just preaching the message but also living it: actually moving house to the places where God's word is needed and living out your faith. The teams of people on the Eden Project did just that, living and working in some of the toughest areas of Manchester, not just for a year, but for life. It was a vocation.

I hadn't heard about this kind of evangelism for a long time, and it struck a chord with me. I'd been taking my bus onto the streets of Southampton to catch up with young people in the places where they were hanging out with their friends, the sort of kids who wouldn't go to a church youth club if you paid them. Now here was Andy talking about living life alongside the kids on the estates of Manchester. I caught his vision, and it made perfect sense to me. The Bus Ministry was planned to support the Eden teams; the bus would provide a sort of mobile youth centre which could visit areas where there was nowhere for kids to meet up.

I wondered if this was the next step for me. Andy said he felt that God was telling him I was the man they wanted – but it was no good unless I felt it as well. I asked for time to talk to Gillian, to think and pray with her about it.

One of the first things I did was to go up and visit The Message in Manchester – I knew I had to see it to understand the nature of the work. I stayed in one of the Eden Project houses, on one of the deprived estates, and I had a good look round and talked to some of the volunteers. At the time I was working with churches in the New Forest, where there were some very well-off areas with posh houses and tree-lined streets – a far cry from the scruffy social housing and concrete walkways of the Manchester estates. I came to the conclusion that the only difference was that in Manchester, what you see is what you get. The area looked poor and deprived, and it was. In the New Forest in the affluent south, there might be a bit more money about, but this often disguised the real problems. People might not be out of work or short of money, but so many of them were still short of love. Kids still went off the rails and experimented with drink and drugs. Housing was more expensive, so young people stood no chance of being able to afford a home of their own. Often they were disillusioned and displaced, with no sense of community.

In any case, wherever you get people, you get similar problems. Family break-ups, drink and drug problems, loneliness, unemployment, a sense that no one cares – these are the same wherever you live. The difference in Manchester was that there was more poverty and a higher crime rate – whatever the causes, the two tend to map together pretty closely. It made life on the estates all the more challenging.

I found out a bit about The Message, too. It started in 1988, when Andy and his brother ran their first youth mission. They had a vision to reach the young people in Manchester for God, and using the biggest rock venue in the city seemed to be a successful way of doing it. Then Mark Pennells, a friend of Andy's, came along. He had been in a band, but had become disillusioned with record deals and big gigs, and he wanted to use his musical gift to share Jesus. Together they set up 'The Message to Schools', doing school assemblies and lunchtime concerts and preaching in the evening – Mark doing the music and Andy preaching. The band evolved, with Andy adding some rapping. They got some people in to sing and some dancers as well, and in 1991 'The World Wide Message Tribe' was born.

The Tribe got more and more successful, but their priority was always the schools in Manchester. Even when they had big recording contracts and were known all over the Christian world, they went on performing in the toughest schools. Once they turned down the chance to perform to 70 million people on international TV, because they were booked to play at a school in Ramsbottom!

One year they ran a mission in Wythenshawe, in south Manchester, and at the end of two weeks they gave a fantastic concert where around 100 kids responded to the gospel. The mission team did what they always did – referred them to the local church – and all 100 turned up on the Sunday! Unfortunately, it was a tiny church of about twenty people – faithful Christians, but quite unable to cope with discipling those numbers. Especially when they were ordinary kids with no church background, whose habits and approach were poles apart from the church. A few of the young people stuck with it, but most of them drifted away.

Andy and the others could see what the problem was: the toughest areas of the city, where the problems and the needs were greatest, were also the areas with the fewest Christians. Any mission they ran in these challenging areas of deprivation, hardship and crime would face the same problem: not enough churches to carry on the long-term work once the mission was over. What was needed was a task force, but not one that went in and out again. They needed groups of Christians who would live and work in those districts. It took a lot of planning and preparation, but the first Eden Project was set up in Wythenshawe in 1997.

Others followed, and they have all been different in minor ways, but they all have four basic elements in common: they're rooted in a local church; they're focused on the toughest neighbourhoods; they include a large team of Christians who are willing to establish their homes in the heart of the community; and they make young people their top priority.

The teams are not professional evangelists: they are ordinary people, living out their ordinary lives in their new communities. They aren't paid: they have to find jobs and housing, just like their neighbours. The difference is that they are Christians, so they find ways to help their community through social action and preaching and living the gospel.

What happened in a short space of time was that

crime rates in Wythenshawe fell, the atmosphere of the neighbourhood improved and even house prices began to rise. The local police spotted the trend straight away and realized that some of the most active young troublemakers on their patch had found something that was drawing them away from crime. The church was making a difference.

Since then eight other Eden Projects have been started, all in deprived and volatile areas where drug and alcohol abuse, gangs, fighting, crime and other social problems abound. The idea of a mobile youth centre where young people could meet their friends, listen to music, watch DVDs and talk to Christian volunteers, seemed like a brilliant way of supporting the work. I came home from Manchester really excited.

It was certainly looking like a job I would love to do, but I couldn't make that decision alone. I had my family to consider, and Gillian and I make all our plans together. We sat down to pray about it.

One of the great things about our marriage is also one of the most difficult things – we have both had our own ministries from the start. Gillian has her ministry as a vicar, while mine is for outreach, in my role as a youth worker, but we both have the same heart for taking the gospel of Jesus to the people who need him, whether in the church or on the street. Occasionally (as in the non-alcoholic bar we established at our church in Southampton) our activities overlap, and we find ourselves working side by side. The rest of the time our ministries and activities are different, though our aims are the same. In our busy schedules, we struggle to make time to be together.

Before we had children, sustaining two ministries was fine. Afterwards it became more of a challenge. Gillian's Director of Training in Southampton once suggested to her that as a mum of two children, maybe she should stay at home and just support me in my work. She replied, 'That sounds lovely, but it isn't what God has asked me to do. Most of the time I would really love to be at home all day – but I know God has put me here to do this job, and I'll go on doing it as best I can.'

It has always meant that we live in a fairly high-pressure world, but we know this is where God wants us to be. Often in Southampton I felt it would be nice if we could spend Friday or Saturday evenings together, like most couples – but in youth work those are the most important nights. We never had much in the way of evenings together, even at weekends. But as Gillian said, philosophically, 'It's one of those things you do for God, really.' We were both busy and committed to giving our lives to God, and we did the best we could to support each other and make sure that the girls got a fair share of our time.

Right now, everything seemed to be coming together. I went through The Message's thorough interviewing system, and a couple of days later Andy Hawthorne rang me to confirm the offer of the job. Gillian and I could see that Manchester would be a good place for both of us, and God had done what he had promised – he had sorted us out two jobs in the same place. I was going to be the Eden Bus Manager, and Gillian was going to be the part-time priest-in-charge of a church in a small town on the edge of

Manchester. We would be living in a vicarage that was close enough to The Message for me to travel to work.

We had mixed feelings about leaving Southampton. Of course we were excited about what God had in store for us, but at the same time we would be sad to leave so many good friends, and the work we had been building up for the last few years. I was happy to be going back up north – even if it was the wrong side of the Pennines! – but Gillian had always lived in the south of England, apart from her time at Edinburgh University. I wondered how different she would find it.

It had never mattered much to me where I lived, because I never had any family base, so I had no one to visit. Most of Gillian's family lived in Cambridgeshire, so the journey from Manchester to visit them wouldn't be much different from the journey from Southampton. Gillian's real sadness was leaving her grandma and grandad, who lived relatively close to us in Portsmouth, so we had been able to visit them quite regularly. They would miss seeing us and their great-granddaughters. I was sad to leave them, too. When I first met them, they really weren't sure what to make of me, but they got to know me and we got on really well. Grandma once said to me, 'You're like a grandson to me,' and that acceptance meant a lot. She was so proud when my first book was published that she told everyone about it! I'm so glad she and grandad were able to read it and be proud of me before they died.

Still, everything else was falling into place. We packed ourselves up and set off for the north. The next phase in our family life was beginning.

Chapter 3

SETTLING IN

Our move was just as mad as our lives always seemed to be. We set off with all our belongings packed in the removal vans, and two very excited little girls in the back of the car. Leah and Natalie were four and two, and they didn't fully understand what a big change was happening in all our lives – all they knew was that it was a very long journey.

We got as far as Winchester when the exhaust started making a very strange noise, and we realized that we needed urgent repairs. We drove the car to a garage and begged them to fix it – and they agreed, since it was clear that we were en route somewhere, with the car filled to bursting with boxes and bags. We gathered the girls and stood watching from a safe distance as the mechanic raised the car onto a ramp over the inspection well. Then we heard the most terrible yowling, so loud that the mechanic stopped the lifting mechanism, because he thought an animal had somehow been run over. It was our cat Louis, still in his cat box on the back seat, and protesting at the strange sensation of going up in a lift! We rescued him, got the car mended and went on our way northwards, much delayed.

Our first impressions were that we were moving to a beautiful area. Our new home was just on the edge of Manchester, and we passed through some wonderful countryside, with high, wild-looking hills and moorland, before we reached the town set in a valley. It was an old mill town, and though some of the warehouses had been converted into smart modern flats, the town itself was still a very ordinary, mostly working-class area. It had chip-shops and pubs and a railway line, with steep streets of grey stone cottages and small brick houses.

The other thing we noticed very quickly was the climate. People had told me it always rained in Manchester, and I didn't believe them – but they were right! It seemed to rain almost every day that autumn. The weather came straight in off the Atlantic, and the clouds dropped all their rain on us before setting off across the Pennines to the rest of the country.

Unfortunately, it turned out that the house we had been allocated by the diocese wasn't in Gillian's new parish at all. For complicated reasons to do with the movement of clergy, another family was living in the vicarage in our parish. We had to be housed temporarily in a different vicarage four miles away, which wasn't an ideal arrangement for a new vicar trying to get to know the church family. Gillian had to travel to the church for services and meetings, some of her new congregation felt abandoned because their vicar wasn't living locally, and it was specially difficult to become a part of 'our' community. Meanwhile, some of the local people resented us being in 'their' vicarage, as we weren't serving their parish. It was to be three years before we moved on, but it was hard to put down roots because we always thought we would move soon. Still, it was a pleasant house and we did our best to settle in. It was a strange sort of 'limbo' time, waiting to move into our real new home, at the heart of the parish where Gillian needed to be.

This arrangement also meant that Leah couldn't start school in our new parish, because technically we were living outside the catchment area. We thought that perhaps this might be a good thing. Gillian would automatically be a governor of the church school, and would be going in to lead assemblies and so on, and Leah might find it embarrassing to have her mum around as the vicar of her school! Fortunately we found another school for her nearby, and it turned out to be a very popular and sought-after church school.

Eventually the good news arrived – the vicarage in our own parish was free. It was right next to the church, so we would be on the spot for all activities and services.

Meanwhile, we'd all been getting used to our new surroundings. I well remember when I first left Yorkshire and moved south: people used to take the mickey out of my accent and pretend not to under-stand me. Now Gillian was the one who was a novelty: she only had to open her mouth and people would say, 'She's not a northerner, is she?' (In fact, these days she has acclimatized quite well, and a few northern phrases have even crept into her sermons!) But I can walk into a shop and say, 'Hello, love,' and no one bats an eyelid. People also called her, jokingly, a 'southern softy' because she was always complaining about the cold. There were one or two strange things with the local language that made us laugh: Gillian was puzzled by people who said, 'Can I give you a lift?' when they knew she had her own car and could drive herself anywhere she wanted. It was a long while before someone explained that in the north, this meant 'Can I give you a hand? Do you want some help?'

Our new church was tiny, with a congregation of around twenty on an average week. They were prayerful people, which was wonderful, and they had managed to keep going in spite of their small numbers and the threat of merging and losing their own minister. They were used to very traditional services, and we could see that there would be some hard decisions ahead. Gillian had a vision for this tiny church. She could see that it wasn't meeting the needs of people in the area – there would have been more people coming to church if it was – yet those traditional services were the preferred form of worship for that faithful remnant of people who had kept the church going for years. We both have a strong urge for mission, and a belief that the church should be spreading the good news of Jesus to everyone. That means reaching out to the unchurched majority – and those are the very people to whom traditional church services mean very little.

We prayed together about our new church family and Gillian's responsibilities. Her vision was for a church where everyone was welcome, an honest place where everyone could grow and learn together. How could she go about meeting the needs of the people within the church, but at the same time reach out and meet the needs of those outside?

Back in Manchester I reported for duty at The Message, not at all sure what was going to be expected of me. For one thing, I didn't know how to drive a bus, so I had to learn. I didn't need a PSV (Passenger Service Vehicle) licence, since we weren't going to carry passengers, but I did need some intensive instruction in how to handle a large vehicle. The bus is forty feet long and eight feet wide, and it weighs around fourteen tonnes. It's not an easy thing to drive, and I spent a hair-raising weekend manoeuvring round the city streets, reversing, going round tight corners and learning to park in a city where I didn't know my way around. It's hard enough to drive a car or ride a bike round Manchester, let alone drive a monster like that. It was such a relief when my instructor told me that I'd passed the test, and I drove back to the office in high spirits.

At that time The Message was located in an old warehouse in Cheadle, which we shared with some other organizations. Our offices were upstairs, and mine was by the fire escape and some rather smelly toilets, so it wasn't exactly glamorous. Still, I had a photo taken with Andy and the team to send to the kids in Southampton. They had been very excited about my new job, thinking I was going to be famous, and saying, 'John's going to work with the Tribe!' I had to keep saying, 'No, I'm going to work for The Message – it's a lot bigger than just the Tribe,' but of course the band was the big thing in their eyes.

In fact The Message was getting bigger: the Eden

teams were in place and growing, and the schools work was increasing too, and it all needed staff to make the arrangements and handle the administration. As the work got bigger, our office space felt smaller: when all twenty-five of us met together for prayer, it was 'Open all the windows and sit on someone's lap!'

Another complication was that although we had a bus – a huge red double-decker – we didn't have anywhere to garage it on site. We had to park it in a haulage yard about fifteen miles away, and that meant a lot of travelling to and fro. I had to learn to be more organized: it was no good going out to work on the bus and then finding I'd left something important in the office.

The story of that first bus was a fascinating one. John and Rose Lancaster are a wonderful couple, vibrant Christians and long-term supporters of The Message. John is a businessman who is known for his faithful charitable giving. They had attended a fundraising dinner at the Manchester United Football Club, where they had heard Andy speaking about his vision for The Message and the projects planned for the next few years. One of them was the Bus Ministry. He described how it would work, and how a bus would enable The Message to get out on the streets and provide youth-club-style facilities to kids who wouldn't normally get the chance to enjoy them. He told them that the bus would support the Eden teams by drawing in the local youngsters, and would give the volunteers the opportunity to share the gospel and show them the love of Christ. Andy realized it might be a while before this dream could become a reality, of course, because it would cost a lot – in the region of £90,000. He hoped that the fund-raising dinner would take a step – however small – towards achieving that dream.

The idea rang bells for John and Rose. They knew how great the needs were in Manchester, and they loved the idea of bringing the youth work to the young people instead of expecting them to conform to the old-fashioned 'church youth club' pattern. They looked at each other, and John got to his feet.

'I've got a bit of a confession to make,' he began, in his blunt northern accent. 'We've been busy for the last couple of weeks – so busy that I forgot to buy my wife a birthday present! But Andy's given me an idea. I think I'll buy her a bus! Go ahead and get your bus, Andy. And we'll cover the cost.'

He was as good as his word: funds were transferred to The Message and the big double-decker bus was duly purchased. Rose was thrilled – especially when she came down to the yard to see 'her' bus, and found that we'd fixed to the bonnet a specially made number plate with the word 'ROSIE' on it! All we had to do now was fit it out.

The budget was better than anything I had ever dreamed of back in the days of my little camper van in Southampton. A whole team of us got together to work out what we wanted, what we needed, what was practical and what wasn't. For instance, we decided that we couldn't have a toilet on the bus (useful though that would have been for us), because it would have to be a chemical toilet, and we'd have to drive to a depot every night to empty it. And anyway, for the bus to be a safe environment, it was important that it was a single open space, with nowhere for anyone to hide or be out of sight. A toilet would be the one place where you couldn't see what the young people might be doing.

The team working on the project included not only staff from The Message but also volunteers who gave their time and expertise generously to help us. They included everyone from designers, computer experts and graphic artists to sheet-metal workers. Everyone's skills were needed, because it was a massive project – it took us around six months to get the bus fully fitted out.

Upstairs we had a massive TV screen, so that it looked like a cinema, with big Bosch speakers and some smaller screens at the back. Below the main screen was a metal rack holding DVDs, CDs and mini-disc players. Downstairs we had X-boxes, Playstations and more plasma screens, and a massive sound system. We also put in a large generator (we started with two small ones but they kept overheating, so we replaced them), a kettle, a microwave, a small office, drinks machines, security cameras, and plenty of storage space. We didn't have anything that could just be picked up and taken away, because we didn't want to get into any difficulties with theft.

We also had to plan how we were going to use the bus once we had it. Andy's original idea had been that we should use the bus to support the work of the Eden teams. On Friday nights we would drive down to one of the team areas, such as Openshaw or Wythenshawe, and meet up with the team. We would pray together about the evening's work, and then we'd open the bus and let the young people on. It was a great contact point for meeting them. Before we took the bus to a new area I would go out with the local Eden team members to get the views of the young people, and I always made contact with the police and local council too.

We did schools work as well, going into schools during the day and plugging the presence of the bus in their area that evening. I used to stand up in the lesson and say, 'Hi, I'm John and I'm a Christian.' Quite often I'd get the reply, 'You don't look like a Christian,' and that would open up a discussion. 'What does a Christian look like? Does it matter what you look like? Does God care what you look like?' They generally got quite involved in talking to me and were keen to see more of what we were offering. One of the gifts God has given me is the ability to relate to young people from all walks of life. As a result, there was always a crowd of youngsters waiting for us when the bus pulled in.

It all added up to a lot of work. I would be working at The Message five days a week, plus the evenings I was driving the bus, and occasionally other times. I was handling the admin associated with the bus; preparing talks, visiting churches and getting other people fired up about the potential of this direct ministry to young people; training the teams in all the issues connected with youth work (from handling aggressive behaviour to child protection law); visiting schools; and then taking the bus project out on the streets.

Gillian was working hard, too. The numbers in the church were small, so in the beginning there was much less pastoral work than there is now. On the other hand, she wanted to focus on evangelism and to enable the church to grow, so some changes were going to be needed. About a year after we had settled in at our new church, while she was still grappling with the problem of moving the church forward, she went on a retreat. As she was praying for the church family, she felt that she had a clear word from God, telling her how she could fulfil both parts of her vision for them. She was to retain their beloved traditional service, but to hold it at 9 a.m. on a Sunday morning. Then she was to start a new, informal 'seeker' service at 10.30, which would become the main service. This would be designed for people who weren't used to coming to church, and would have plenty of variety and interest, with modern music and an approachable style.

Obediently, she put this plan into action, and together we entered a difficult time of change. A few people didn't like the new arrangements, and a couple of folk left the church entirely. It was particularly painful for Gillian, because she came in for a lot of personal criticism for that – apparently driving away some of the few church members she had, who had been there for a long time. The numbers attending the early service declined, until at the lowest point there were only about three people coming to that service regularly. Other ministers might have given it up at that stage, but Gillian was sure that it was an important part of God's plan, so she persevered, and gradually the numbers picked up. As new people joined the church, some of them decided that they liked the quiet early service and chose that as the main focus for their worship.

All the same, it was a difficult time for us, and we found it emotionally quite stressful to know that so many of the congregation didn't like what we were doing. Gillian tried to explain that she wanted people to grow, and that she didn't believe that God had put her there simply to care for a tiny congregation, but we knew that behind our backs many people were complaining about all the changes. I found it particularly hard: I'd had so much rejection in the past that I was acutely sensitive to criticism. We had to accept that we couldn't please everyone all the time, because often what some people want from you is the direct opposite of what others want!

We were getting some stress from the pace of life, too. Gillian was fitting caring for the girls around her work as a vicar, while I had to work some weekends as part of my job. We have some very dear friends who help and counsel us, and it's always good to hear an objective view. Gillian's mentor Shirley was very helpful over this, and it was she who pointed out that although we were carefully prioritizing time for the girls, we also needed to make time for ourselves as a couple. Another day our friend Sue said to me, 'John, you've done ninety hours this week. What on earth do you think you're doing? Where does your family come in all this?' She was right to make me stop and think. It was time for another look at our diary, and time to try to cut back where we could. Our family is a gift from God, and a priority.

I found it difficult. When I'm working I get immersed in what we're doing, and in the lives of the young people we meet. I know how much difference we're making, and I want so much to help them and give them the chance to meet Jesus and know him as their Lord.

It's a constant juggling act, but Sue's advice was timely: 'It's God first, then your family, and then your work.' Even if the work is God's, we try to keep to that order, because although we have a responsibility to preach the gospel to the young people in Manchester, and to our church family, we have even more responsibility to teach and care for our own two lovely girls. We don't want them to grow up thinking that mummy and daddy had time for the church and not for them. So we try to programme in fun family time together, and to make sure that one of us is always there to tell them a bedtime story and put them to bed. With no family background of my own, building a Christian family is another thing I've had to learn from scratch.

Chapter 4

A GOOD NIGHT OUT

My job is pretty varied, but my main activity is running the Bus Ministry. A typical night out on the bus follows a pattern: we meet up with the team and pray for around half an hour; then we drive to the location where we'll be working and run the evening session for two to three hours; at the end we drive off, stop and have another prayer time and a debrief on the events of the evening; and then we drive the bus back to the garage and go home. However, 'typical' is never a word I'd use, because within that framework, every night is different.

When we meet up with the team for the area we're going to, we always have a chat about the local issues first. There may be some young people who have been barred from the bus (this happens occasionally if there are issues with aggression and violence), or particular events like gang fights or shootings that we need to be aware of. I allocate people to designated areas of the bus, four upstairs and four downstairs, with two people on the door, working always in mixed pairs, so there's always a male and a female together.

We also need to have our prayer time together, and hand over the whole evening to God. We do this first, before we drive to our location, so that we can do it in peace. Once, back in the early days, we parked up and sat down for our prayer time, even though there was already a group of youngsters waiting for us to open the doors. We finished praying and looked up to see, through the bus windows, a whole row of bare bums: the kids had got bored waiting and decided to moon at us! Other times we've been disturbed by kids shouting and swearing and sticking their fingers up at us, so we've learned to have our prayer time elsewhere, without disturbance.

Then we start up the generators, put the music on and open the doors. Generally the kids have seen the bus coming and they're already queuing up outside. Most of them are between the ages of nine and seventeen, though if we have too many to fit on the bus we sometimes split up the evening, and have the younger ones on at the start and the older ones later on.

After that, anything can happen! Some of them want to play with X-boxes and Playstations (although many of them have this stuff at home); we may show a film or play music. We're always careful if they bring their own DVDs or CDs, and check that they're appropriate, because we want to give out a consistent Christian message. Sometimes they play games, and often they just want to sit and talk with us and their friends – on a cold winter's night a warm, brightly lit bus is a better place to be than a dark street corner.

Our job is to be there for them, to engage with them and listen to them. We accept them as they are, because that's how God accepts them, but at the same time we have to make the bus a safe environment for everyone, so we have to have some ground-rules. We don't allow anyone on if they've been drinking too much or taking drugs – we monitor the kids carefully and can usually tell if they've had too much, and we have to make decisions on the spot. I've had young people smoking cannabis, and I've said to them, 'You're making it so obvious that you're taking drugs, and yet you want to come on the bus. Make up your mind which you want to do.'

If they're tooled up with a gun or a knife we ask them to leave – and we're prepared to restrain them if they kick off and have a go at any of the team. We make sure that everyone is fully trained to use minimum force to defend themselves. We've also had interesting incidents with BB guns being used to show off and scare people, but they can be as dangerous as real guns.

We have to take these precautions, but we do it unobtrusively, because we want the evening to be relaxed, so that the young people can meet the team and relate to each other. We have a great time playing games with some of the toughest cookies in the neighbourhood. If they come on wearing hoodies we get them to take the hood down. We don't have a problem with hoods but they hide your face, and on the bus we like the security cameras to pick up the faces – just in case.

Security cameras may sound a bit severe, but they're there for everyone's protection: if anything does go down (as it has on a number of occasions), we are able to produce the video evidence. For instance, one night a lad was told to leave the bus, and he accused the driver of hitting him and physically dragging him off the bus. The police happened to come by on a routine patrol, and he went over and told them he'd been assaulted. The police officer came back with him and spoke to me. 'We appreciate the work you're trying to do here,' she said. 'But if he's really been assaulted, you know I'll have to act accordingly.'

I was standing in the doorway of the bus, and I turned to the boy and said, 'OK, lad, I appreciate what you're saying. One of my team members will get into serious trouble if you continue with this allegation. You're entitled to do that. But I just want you to know that we've got the whole evening on video, so if you want to change your story, now would be a good time to do it.'

The boy looked over my shoulder and noticed the CCTV camera for the first time. We can't print what he said, but he decided that he didn't want to make the accusation.

It's hard to convey how volatile these situations can be. We see plenty of young people who behave fine and have no particular problems – they just want to have fun with their friends, and they'll have a laugh and a chat and enjoy being on the bus. But in these very deprived areas where crime rates are high, violence can be a way of life, and we have to be prepared. After seventeen years' experience in youth work, you get to know when something is about to kick off.

There was one lad who got really angry about something and smashed his fist through one of the plasma screens. I told him he was barred from the bus until he apologized. I never said anything about paying for the damage – they're huge things and very expensive, and I knew he could never afford to pay for it – but I wanted him to know that there had to be boundaries, and he had to be responsible for his actions. He just swore and said, 'I'm not doing that!' – so he's still barred. I'll allow him back if he apologizes and recognizes that he has done something wrong. It costs a lot of money to maintain our buses, and a lot of that is given prayerfully by people who don't have much themselves. We need to lead the young people to recognize that.

At the end of the evening we have the God Slot. We don't give anyone the choice of staying downstairs and continuing to play computer games or music, but they don't have to come to the God Slot, either: they can come upstairs and join in with the story and prayer time or they can leave the bus. We close down all the activities and say 'It's up or off!' We regularly have between thirty-five and sixty young people coming upstairs to join in.

First, one of the team will stand up and share their testimony. People often say to me, 'My testimony's not like yours, John,' and I say, 'I wouldn't want it to be. I wouldn't want you to have my past.' But everyone has a testimony, because it's the story of their encounter with God. When we let Christ into our lives, we're all equal.

The kids often start out with a bit of heckling, shouting and swearing, but once they've got over that, they realize that we've got something to share, and they love it. They love having the person in front of them, and they listen to the stories because they know they're true. At the end, they ask loads of questions.

We try to balance the questions with their prayer requests, and we get a lot of them. Kids will say, 'Will you pray for my auntie...or uncle...or friend.' Some of their requests are quite funny. We've had boys ask us to pray that they will get a girlfriend, 'and she has to look like this...' and they give us a detailed specification! Some of the requests are quite sad, but we take them all seriously. If a kid asks us to pray that they'll win the lottery, we say, 'God knows your heart. He knows what you really need. Do you really need to win the lottery?' If anyone really refuses to be serious, we ask them to leave, because it can be offensive when other people are talking about things that matter deeply to them. We often have eight or ten young people coming forward at the end for more prayer, or to talk seriously about whether they're ready to accept Christ into their lives.

If we have a kid who's swearing offensively about God, I sometimes say, 'I dare you to come forward and pray this prayer, because it takes a lot of courage. It takes a real man or woman to stand up and say, "Lord, I know I've done wrong and I want to give my life to you."' I don't have a problem with issuing a challenge like this: only the Holy Spirit knows what work he is doing in people's hearts, and we never know what life will hold for these young people. Sadly, some of those who used to come to our bus are no longer with us – they've died in different situations.

We always pray, 'Lord, please let your Holy Spirit work on this bus. We want to see miracles and we want to see lives being changed.' We have seen some amazing responses, and not just after months of work

– sometimes it's when we move into a new area. If God's going to do it, he will. We don't need to be there for six months before anything can happen. You never know what will make a difference to people, or what will enable them to open up sufficiently to admit their need for faith.

There was one group of youngsters from the Weaste project who were regulars on the bus, and they'd heard me talking about Lee Abbey. I said, 'Maybe we can go for a weekend away some time,' and they were really keen. A lot of these young people have never been out of Manchester, so a trip to Devon was exciting for them. Along with three helpers, I took twelve of them for a residential weekend, and a pretty wild time it turned out to be! We had to take alcohol off them before they got onto the bus, and even then they managed to smuggle about £100 worth of spirits in their luggage. They couldn't believe how far it was, and once we were out in the countryside they looked around in amazement. 'Where are the shops? Where are the pubs?' they kept asking, as if they couldn't believe that anyone could possibly live outside the city.

The journey took about eight hours. It would have been quicker if I hadn't had to pull over and stop so often, because they kept taking their seat belts off, messing about and throwing food. Their behaviour was pretty bad, considering we were doing something for their enjoyment. When we finally arrived at Lee Abbey we went to the Beacon Youth Centre and took them to their rooms. They were blown away by the place, and by the little chocolates and prayer cards left on their pillows to welcome them. It didn't make much difference to their behaviour, though.

We had a terrible time trying to get them up for breakfast. That was because they'd been up till about 4 a.m., smoking and drinking vodka. I challenged them that if they kept drinking they would have to leave, so they dutifully lined up and handed in their vodka bottles. The staff were impressed by their obedience, but I was suspicious when I noticed how wobbly they were. I opened the bottles and sniffed, and sure enough, they'd filled them with water. They'd emptied out the vodka by drinking it, and I was quite concerned about how fast they'd managed to dispose of it, but they didn't seem to suffer any ill effects.

The wild behaviour went on all weekend, as they were introduced to all sorts of 'adventure' activities. The archery was a popular option, but of course they weren't bothered about the targets, and I had my work cut out trying to stop them shooting each other. Then one evening, in the discussion session, a girl called Naomi from Lee Abbey gave her testimony. She came from a similar background to them, and she'd had similar issues with self-worth. The whole group seemed unusually quiet and subdued, and one or two of the girls had tears in their eyes. At the end of the session, as we stood up to leave, two of the young people went over and hugged her – not the sort of thing they would normally do. I felt it was a real breakthrough, and worth all the hard work and the nightmare of trying to keep them under some sort of control.

After that they kept asking if we could go away

again. I knew they'd seen something, and felt something, that they'd never met before: a level of caring and honesty that made them feel valued. Six months later one of these lads became a Christian on the bus.

Many of the young people we've worked with stay in my mind. Some of them have come through; they've gone into the army or the police, got a job, set up their own businesses, got married and settled down. Sadly, some of the others end up in prison and we go and visit them there. In *Nobody's Child* we printed a letter from Sara, who was sixteen when she was sent to prison for kidnapping and wounding. She said that she had written down 'some things about what it's like in here to try and stop kids from getting into trouble before it's too late...if you get the chance to, please read it to them because I don't want them to end up like me.' We kept in touch and I believe that God supported her through her sentence. Once someone has chosen to open the door to God, we see time after time how he never lets them go.

When we're chatting to the young people throughout the evening we're doing real youth work, gaining an insight into their lives, their worries and concerns, as they talk to us about anything from having a family to what they call 'religion'. The bus can be really buzzing with music and noise, but at the end of the night it's fantastic to hear them talking seriously about prayer without having to joke about it. When they've had real, honest interactions with people, they lose some of their defensive edginess because we've built up trust. They know the team members are real, ordinary, honest people who care about them.

There was one young girl who used to come along and always kick off about something, because there was so much anger in her. You could see from her eyes that she was really hurting inside, and it came out as aggression. She used to thump me on the shoulder and call me 'gayboy' and other names. Yet at the end of the night she would look at me pleadingly and say, 'You will come back next week, won't you?' In spite of all her aggression, she had picked up on the fact that the people on the bus cared about her.

That's why this work is so demanding: we have to be there for these young people, and often the most difficult ones are the most damaged ones who need our special care. I always say to our volunteers that they can't come along and take it easy. 'If you're too tired one night, just stay at home.' They have to be open and available and responsive, because you never know what baggage the kids are bringing in with them.

One night I was standing at the door of the bus and another of our regulars came up. She was a bright young girl, and she was usually quite loud and lairy, but she seemed a bit subdued.

I said, 'How are you?'

She said, 'Yeah, I'm all right.'

'No, really – how are you?'

'Well...not too good, really.'

I could have let it go, and I didn't want to push her, so I just said, 'Well, if you want to talk about it...'

Then she said quietly, 'Well, I came home tonight and my dad was hanging in the stairwell.'

She was trying to deal with her dad's suicide, and

if I hadn't made that extra effort to speak to her, I couldn't have given her that opening.

You never know what's going to happen, and you never know what the story will be. Often it's to do with loss – an illness, a shooting, a fight or a separation. Sometimes I just want to cry for them, because I can see what's missing in their lives. They long for love and security. If we listen to them, we can give them the space to offload some of their fear and loneliness in safe surroundings.

We take the buses to different areas of Manchester, where there are different teams of volunteers waiting for us, and we see the same quality of relationships being built up every time. Back at The Message we have a project called Genetik, where young people aged eighteen and over from different countries come to work with us. They spend time with The Tribe Academy doing music, they do schools work and prison work, and they join us on the bus. We use a lot of these guys when they're doing a six-month placement, where they live together in a house in an Eden team area. They're a great resource because they have passion, enthusiasm, energy and vision – and I add some training so that they are able to work on the streets with us.

There was one German girl whose English (fortunately) wasn't very good, and a guy went up to her on the bus and was being very aggressive, telling her what he'd like to do to her. I went up and told him he was out of order: 'We don't talk to you like that, so don't talk to a member of my staff like that.' I asked him to leave the bus. Karin asked me what he'd said, and I just said, 'He liked you – he liked you a lot.' That was all she needed to know. These young Christians have such a witness, they've put themselves on the front line for Jesus, and they're learning as they go along, but we have to protect them some of the time.

Teamwork is very important, and we have to support each other. It's quite a stressful and demanding situation to be in, and we're alert all the time. You're like a coiled spring, ready for anything, being aware of what's going on all around, and never letting your guard down. If a situation is starting to develop, we always give the young people a warning. 'Guys, please don't swear and shout.' The second time we say, 'If we have to tell you again you'll have to leave.' The third time we take action and they must leave the bus – and it's important that we follow through consistently, so everyone knows the score. It always works OK and I've never had a volunteer badly injured, even though there is sometimes some violence. We use a traffic-light response: green is OK, amber is a high alert, because there's the potential for something going down, and red is action stations, because something is happening.

We keep in touch using walkie-talkies rather than mobile phones, which are all locked away – you don't want to have anything on you that can be stolen – and we use a lot of sign language instead of saying things out loud. We monitor the whole bus closely all the time, with staff at the back, middle and front on both floors, keeping an eye on things. This isn't overkill. We work in some of the toughest areas of Greater Manchester, where drug-related crime and drive-by shootings are not just things you see in American cop movies – they're regular occurrences. We've had guys dealing drugs from their cars on the next street corner. Sometimes they have driven by and given us the 'gun' sign, because they want to get at the kids on the bus and deal stuff to them.

It's a privilege to work with the young people who live in these tough areas, not least because we know what a big effect we can have on their lives. The kids know we work in partnership with the police, so we aren't an escape from the law, but they know we don't repeat everything they tell us, apart from where we are bound by the law. The police support us (with finance as well) because they're so pleased with the response to our work. When we have up to 150 kids around the bus of an evening, the crime rate drops, because some of the young offenders are in the crowd listening to our music and not out nicking cars. The police also act with some sensitivity to make sure they don't break down the trust we're building up. If they want to arrest someone they won't do it on the bus, even if they know that's the best place to find them. They speak to them elsewhere.

It's important that we use the local teams who understand their areas and the sometimes volatile situations that can arise. Once we saw a nasty fight between two lads. One guy came from another patch and he hit a boy with a metal bar. The boy's dad came along and made the two boys fight it out. We pleaded with him and said, 'Why make them fight?' He replied, 'This is a tough area. If he doesn't stick up for himself he won't survive.' We had to try to understand his attitude – in a place where the culture was one of violence, he was trying to prepare his son for the reality of life as he saw it. We might be totally against violence, but we were going into their community and we needed to understand their culture and respect it. All we could do was pray that no one would get hurt.

At the end of the evening we wind up the God Slot with prayer, especially with any of the young people who have been affected by what's been said. Sometimes that effect is handed on to their family. They can have a little Gideon Bible, so their parents can see that we're not wacky Christians trying to brainwash their kids. One night a man sat at the back of the bus because he had come to collect his son, and he was in tears at the end of the God Slot. He came and asked us to pray with him, too.

We've had kids who used to come along to the bus and cause trouble, but now they prepare something for the God Slot and make their own contribution. They will stand up and lead a discussion about how they think God relates to us and speaks to us – it's a big achievement for them to stand up in front of 100 kids and talk like that.

We had one girl who used to come on the bus swearing and arguing with everyone, but gradually she settled down and seemed to appreciate the quiet time at the end of the evening. We gave her a copy of *Nobody's Child*, and she told us that after she'd read it she gave it to her mum, who read it and then passed it on to her uncle. Nowadays this girl behaves quite differently – she's a warm, gentle, respectful person. She brings her mates along to the God Slot and makes a thoughtful contribution.

She's an example of someone gradually inching her way towards faith, and we have quite a few in every area like that. They feel safe enough to join in with the God Slot, and they are actually ministering to others, though they may not themselves have ever stood up and prayed the prayer of acceptance. Maybe it's only later that they will understand their faith properly, but we meet them where they are today, and help them to explore their faith level as it is now.

On the other hand, we have youngsters who understand what we're offering, and show how hungry they are for understanding. In one of our areas there's a vicar who's been doing a lot of work with a group of kids aged eight to twelve. His church is full of activity, and as well as groups for Mums and Toddlers they run after-school clubs and give the kids a safe place to play football. The young people often have behavioural problems – they swear and spit in your face – and it takes a great deal of patience to work with them. A lot of it is learned behaviour: they shout because they're shouted at at home.

In these situations you have to be aware of the culture they're coming from. If you say to these kids, 'I love you and care about you', they'll say, 'He's a pervert' or 'He's gay'. Often there are very few men in their community, and they look up to inappropriate male role models: fighters and drug dealers. That vicar is doing fantastic work with the kids, giving them the sort of tough love that helps them, caring for them but setting boundaries for acceptable behaviour. He knows them all well, and understands what's going on in their lives.

I met one of 'his' kids one day when the bus was open for a fun day. He was a stocky little lad with a cheerful personality, but a bit of a loner with few friends. He looked round the bus and came up to me and said, 'Where's the bus going to be tomorrow?' I told him, and gave him one of the cards we give out, with a picture of the buses and the bus schedule on them. I gave him a card for 'Monday' saying where the bus would be, and he duly turned up for the whole session. At the end, after the God Slot, he said, 'So where will you be tomorrow, then?' So we gave him a card for Tuesday.

Sure enough, he turned up again, and for the whole week he followed the bus round, each day getting a card for the next day's location. At the end of the week he met one of the bus team in the street, stopped him and said, 'I want to be a Christian – how do I do it?' They stood and prayed together on the street corner, with people walking past, and afterwards the lad was really proud of himself. He was actually swaggering and saying, 'Well, I've done it now! I'm a Christian!' He knew what he wanted – even at the age of eleven – and he made sure he got it.

At the end of the prayer time we get all the kids off the bus and close the doors. If there are a lot of kids in the area we have to be very diligent and try to disperse them: sometimes when we pull away we've had young people lie down in front of the bus, or try to hang onto the back. We can't monitor the area after we've gone, but we try to leave a location knowing that the young people have gone, too, and not leave a problem behind us for the residents.

Tired as we are, often we're rejoicing as we drive away. We've seen amazing miracles on the bus, with young people getting to know Jesus. Every week we see at least one person give their life to Christ, and the challenge then is what we do next. The bus isn't a church, and the new Christians need a church that can meet them as we have – where they are, even if that means with a can of beer in one hand and a fag in the other. God can deal with that, but can the congregation? Not every church is geared up to work with young people who aren't used to sitting through a sermon and may be popping out every five minutes for a cigarette. That's where the Eden teams come into their own, because they are already linked with churches who are committed to this work, and are willing to embark on the long process of discipling these needy youngsters.

Meanwhile, we drive off for our time of prayer, then drop off the team members at their cars before the bus driver takes the bus back to The Message. A typical night? I suppose so. Yet every night is different, and everyone we meet is an individual, and only God is always the same, meeting us all where we are, and encouraging us to move on to something better.

Chapter 5

THERE'LL BE ANOTHER ONE ALONG IN A MINUTE!

Around two and a half million people live in Greater Manchester. About half a million of these are young people under the age of eighteen, many of them living in neglected inner-city areas. These are the communities which suffer from high crime, poor health, low educational achievement, a dilapidated environment, broken families and few opportunities. The vast majority of the population knows nothing about the love which God showed for the world through Jesus, and most of them have no interest in religion or traditional church services.

What drew me to The Message was its desire to help the kind of young people I care most about – the lost, deprived ones, who drift into drink, drugs and crime because they can't see anything else to do; those who are rejected like I was, and who feel unloved. Andy Hawthorne had a vision to see young people come to know Jesus, because he knew from personal experience that becoming a Christian transforms lives. I was a good example of that. If God hadn't intervened in my life, I'm pretty sure I wouldn't be here today. I'd have died on the streets through illness or violence or just giving up in despair.

The Message believes that when young people's lives are transformed, their communities can be restored, so by reaching out to the young people of Manchester, it's offering hope and a lifeline to the whole city. Maybe that sounds like a big claim, yet you can see evidence of it all around. A gang of rowdy youths can change the atmosphere of an area. Once vandalism and graffiti and petty crime become more frequent, everyone starts to feel threatened. That sets the stage for gangs to develop, kids start carrying weapons to defend themselves, and maybe the drug dealers move in. By the same token, if some of those key youngsters have somewhere to go, instead of hanging out on street corners; if they stop being bored and start to develop other interests; most of all, if they meet Jesus and let him turn their lives around, then that, too, is infectious. The mood of a whole estate can begin to change.

This was what we saw in the summer of 2000, when Soul Survivor moved up to Manchester. Soul Survivor's core values had always been teaching, worship and ministry, but Mike Pilavachi came to see the work of The Message and realized that they had to add evangelism, the missing dynamic. 'Unless we raise up worshippers,' he said, 'we're not really worshipping.' He decided to cancel Soul Survivor 2000, and moved the entire event to Manchester for ten days of mission. That summer 11,000 people from twenty nations went out into the city, to preach the gospel in word and deed.

That in itself was a staggering achievement, but one particular event really demonstrated what could be done. A policeman called Phil Green had been working on the Swinton Valley Estate, a deprived area with a high crime rate, boarded-up houses, and litter and mess everywhere. He came up with the idea of bringing in a thousand young people to clean the whole place up, clear gardens, do up the Community Centre, and put in a park. All the young people they made contact with on the estate were invited to huge free parties in the Evening News Arena. They worked hard, and the effect was amazing.

For a start, you couldn't move for Christians – young, enthusiastic Christians – and everyone was talking about Jesus. Suddenly it was quite normal to hear people talking about God. Then, the physical changes they brought about were striking: once the place had been cleaned up, it looked completely different. All the residents got involved, and people started to take a pride in their area. The biggest change, though, no one could have predicted. The previous weekend on that estate there had been eleven burglaries and any amount of car crime. During the whole ten days of the mission there were no recorded incidents of crime at all, and in the following months, the police recorded a sustained reduction in crime of 45 per cent.

No one gets involved in outreach work with the aim of reducing crime, but when it happens, it catches the attention of people who wouldn't normally take much interest in the church. The police and the press started to take notice. People began to wonder what made young people give up their time to try to bring help and hope to these communities. For us at The Message, it supported our belief that the way to help was to make reaching the young people our top priority.

That short ten-day mission was unusual. The key to the normal Eden work was something different: sustained, long-term effort. To make a real difference to the lives of the most broken, hurting and hopeless people, you have to be there with them. The Eden Teams make a bold statement by moving into those estates permanently. When people ask them, 'Why have you moved here?' they tell them the truth – they want to help and support the community, because that's what God is telling them to do. They have made a long-term commitment to that neighbourhood. Relationships get established, friendships are built and faith is shared. It's the best possible kind of witness.

It was a privilege to run the Eden Bus Ministry, and to support the guys who have lived and worked in these areas for years, getting to know the young people and their families. We could come in and offer them a safe place to meet, a range of activities and an opportunity to talk about what matters to them. By 2001 there were five Eden Teams in operation, in Salford, Openshaw, Longsight, Swinton and Harpurhey. We were out several nights a week visiting different areas. In fact, we were beginning to struggle – the bus was always in demand, and although we took care to keep it in good condition, from time to time we would have a breakdown, and that would mean letting people down. It was clear that the work couldn't expand much further without a second bus. Having been involved in fitting out the first one, I knew what was involved. The financial implications of the idea were staggering, and we only knew one way to get that sort of money – through prayer. We didn't tell anyone what we were hoping for, we just put it to God. If it was his will for the work to expand, he would show us the way.

One afternoon we were out on the bus in the Weaste area of Salford, and John and Rose Lancaster had come down to see how the work was progressing. Rose was waiting for an operation on her hip, and she was in quite a lot of pain, but she wasn't going to let that stop her visiting us. John and Rose support several charities, and run a medical mission overseas, but they are great believers in what they call 'the ministry of relationships'. They don't believe in just giving money to support causes, because money alone doesn't show people the love of Jesus. All Jesus' ministry was about bringing people to God, and so theirs is a two-fold ministry: meeting needs but also making relationships. They are very active partners in all the work they support, visiting and getting to know the people involved, and encouraging our volunteers with their cheerful friendliness and their down-to-earth understanding of the work we're doing.

This particular afternoon Rose was standing on the pavement as I was talking to a couple of girls in the bus doorway. Just then a lad came along the street on his bike, swerved towards the bus, wobbled a bit and crashed into Rose – and his handlebars struck her on the hip that she was having trouble with. She went white with the pain, and I could see her biting back the tears. She told me afterwards that she wanted to scream as the pain shot down her leg. She grabbed onto the bus door, and after a bit we helped her to climb inside and sit down.

When I got a quiet moment I went in and sat down with her.

'I'm really sorry about that,' I said. 'The lad was really sorry, too – he even apologized!'

'That's all right, John,' she said. 'It's a bit better now – but it got me thinking. I mean, I've got a problem with my hip, but I can get treatment for that, and once I've had my op I'll be OK. I'm in pain at the moment, but it's only temporary. But I've listened to some of these kids' stories, and they're in pain in their whole lives. I heard you talking to those girls – you're so caring, and that's what they need, people to care for them. I could have cried about my hip, but I could cry even more for these kids.

'We've had a bit of a chat, and we think your work's so valuable. Would you like the money for another bus, so you can do more?'

I was staggered. We hadn't mentioned a second bus to anyone – except God, in our regular prayer times. I couldn't believe they could be offering us the whole thing on a plate – especially after their incredible generosity in buying us the first one.

I told them what we'd been praying for. 'Well,' said Rose comfortably, 'sometimes God just gives you a nudge. Sometimes quite hard,' she added, rubbing her hip.

We started looking for another bus at once. It was important that it had a reliable engine as well as sound bodywork. You can build any amount of equipment into a nice-looking bus, but it's no good if the engine dies and it lets you down. I looked in magazines and talked to everyone I knew, hoping someone would hear of something suitable. Then I found an advert for a coach which had once been the Nottingham Forest Football Club tour bus. It looked perfect, and it would be great for long journeys like going to Soul Survivor.

I went to meet the owner, but he wanted £64,000. The price was understandable – the whole thing was kitted out for touring, with seats, tables, a separate unit with showers, and even a bar on the top deck. His price took account of all the fittings, and of course he wasn't to know that we would be ripping them all out and starting again. I offered him £26,000, but he turned me down. 'I might as well give it away,' he said.

I was disappointed, because I'd felt so sure that it was the right bus for us, but I went away and started looking again. The weeks went by, and I didn't find anything to match that first bus. Then, three months later, I got a phone call from the owner. He hadn't managed to sell it, and he was prepared to lower his price. In the end I bought it for my original amount I offered! I drove it back to The Message, feeling increasingly pleased with my bargain. The bus had an automatic Mercedes Benz engine, and was fantastic to drive. Then I got down to the hard work of planning once again.

I sat down with a good friend who works in accounts and we went through everything we would need – the plasma screen, the X-boxes and Playstations, the seating arrangements, even the mobile phones. It was a new experience for me – I had to draw up a budget for about £80,000, and I was a bit nervous when I presented it to John Lancaster. I thought I'd allowed for everything, but John, who is a wise and experienced businessman as well as one of the most generous people I know, looked thoughtful.

'That's fine,' he said. 'But I think we'd better allow a bit extra for contingencies – in case things turn out a bit more expensive than you think.' Bless him, he was right, and we needed the extra. I so appreciated not having to go back to him to ask for a bit more, each time something turned out to cost more than I'd budgeted for.

We made detailed plans. The second bus was going to be different in minor ways from the first: for instance, the location of the generator was changed to make it more vandal-proof. We'd learned some useful lessons from our experience of running Eden Bus 1.

By this time The Message had moved from our cramped quarters in Cheadle to a big office building on an industrial estate. The offices were new and well equipped, and we had room for both of the buses to be parked on our own premises and under cover. I had to learn more about project management, and make sure that every bit of the fitting-out job was done properly and in the right order. It was a real learning curve for me. In the end we had a second fantastic vehicle, fully equipped and professionally spray-painted with our logo and some great graphic design.

We had a big launch party, with the Tribe performing and both buses open for viewing. Everyone was pleased with the end result. The kids climbed on and said 'Wow – it's really cool!' We always have the best and latest technology, not just to impress them, but because they need to see excellence. It makes them feel valued that we are prepared to offer them an environment of this standard. If we can care like this, it's easier to tell them that God loves them, too. Whenever the kids say that the bus is fantastic, I say, 'If you think this is good, think how much more amazing God is.' It was a very exciting time. We were ready to go up a gear with the Bus Ministry.

For one thing, a second bus enabled us to go into schools more often. The Message already had a ministry to schools, doing assemblies and RE lessons, and sometimes running short missions. The bus gave an added dimension. On one recent mission we took the bus along and all the RE lessons that week were conducted on the bus. We did talks on citizenship and self-worth, with lots of quizzes and interactive activities. For instance, we show the kids two pairs of jeans – one comes from Oxfam and costs £2, while the other has an expensive designer label. 'Which one is worth more?' we ask. 'What about the person wearing them – are people worth more because of the clothes they wear?' We show them pictures of well-known faces and ask who is the most valued – David Beckham or Mother Theresa? We do presentations, group work, games and discussion. The students enjoy it because it's something different, in a different environment, and the teachers enjoy it because they can have a lesson off, sit at the back of the bus with a cup of coffee, and catch up on their marking!

Usually we encourage the students to go to the big concert at the end of the week, where there will be a proper presentation of the gospel and an invitation to respond, but on this occasion I just had a feeling that the time was right. I knew that the teacher wasn't a Christian – these days RE is about teaching five major world religions, not about Christianity alone, and teachers do not necessarily have a faith of their own, even if they are RE specialists. I didn't want to offend her, but at the end of the lesson I decided to ask the young people if they wanted Jesus to come into their lives. We had a big class of about forty-five pupils, and to our amazement, twenty-seven kids put up their hands. We gave each of them a Gideon Bible and encouraged them to go to the concert that evening led by Blush, The Message's girl band. I made sure that the Christian teachers in the school followed up that amazing response.

Of course, having another bus meant more work. I was already at full stretch, managing the organization, fund-raising, giving talks, driving the first bus, and even cleaning it. I didn't mind what I did, but I couldn't put in any more hours than I already did, and anyway, I couldn't be in two places at once. We needed more staff. I needed team leaders for each area as well as a mechanic to keep the buses on the road.

Recruiting staff for the Bus Ministry wasn't just a simple matter of advertising for them. We needed people who really cared about the work. You could have the most fantastic bus in the world – it could have a swimming pool on the roof! – but if the staff don't share the vision, it won't work. I often get letters from people saying that they'd like to have a similar bus in their area, but I always tell them the same thing. The key ingredient isn't the equipment or the facilities: it's the Holy Spirit inspiring people with the vision, enthusiasm and commitment for the work.

For instance, you need about forty volunteers. That's because we always have a team of at least eight on the bus at any one time, and as these people have jobs and lives and they need some evenings free, there needs to be a rota. They take it in turns to go out. Even if the bus breaks down and can't go out, those volunteers will still turn up to talk to the kids, at the time and place where the bus would have been. These kids are let down so often, it's really important that they see our faithfulness and commitment to them in this. When the volunteers turn up, it shows that they care for them. We get some strange looks sometimes, when the team is standing there in the pouring rain with hands on each other's shoulders, praying together before a session just as we would if we were on the bus. Sometimes those evenings turn out to be the most effective, because the young people have seen how committed we are as individuals.

By this time, we weren't just going into the Eden Project estates. The Bus Ministry had been recognized by the police, as its effectiveness in reducing crime, juvenile nuisance and anti-social behaviour was proved again and again. It wasn't unusual for the police to make a special request for us to target an area strategically, giving us funding from their crime prevention budget. We weren't going in as crime-busters, though. We never went into an area unless we had done thorough preparation and had the support of the local church to follow up our work.

Often the churches themselves would make the first contact, and ask us to come and give a presentation about the work and tell them how we could work in partnership. I was always realistic about the cost – both personal and financial – and I always explained first and foremost that what they needed was a team of local volunteers, on fire with the gospel and a vision for the work. They needed to go and talk to the young people in the area, and make sure that they thought a visit one night a week by a mobile youth centre would be a good idea. If they didn't want it, it wouldn't come to anything, because they'd just trash the bus. If they did want it, they'd take ownership of it, and then we could get something started.

Once we had the volunteers, there was still a lot to do. We had to get every volunteer police checked, because they would be working with young people. Then I had to train the bus drivers, and when they completed the course they got a certificate saying they were qualified to drive a bus of that size and weight. The drivers were vital, because the best people to take a bus into an area are the people who live there. The kids love it when they see their mums and dads driving our great big bus into their street.

The volunteers don't just have to be drivers – they have to have other gifts, too, because they have to operate as part of the team. Once they've parked up, they lock up the driver's area of the bus and get to work alongside everyone else. I give everyone training on handling aggression – not self-defence, but tips on body language. To do this work you have to understand that you can be a Christian without being treated like a total muppet. Some youths think that because you're a Christian they can spit in your face and swear, and you'll have to take it. With training, people learn that they can be strong and set boundaries for acceptable behaviour without resorting to physical contact.

We treat the young people with respect, but we don't stand for anyone kicking off or spoiling the event for others. Sometimes we have to ask people to leave (for instance, if they're picking fights with other kids or the staff, or if they're smoking or drinking), but we generally manage to do it in a good-humoured way.

There was one night when I made a big mistake. I saw a young lad get onto the bus – where we have a strict no-smoking policy – with a cigarette in his hand, but he tucked it under his coat. I stopped him and said, 'Mate, you're smoking.'

'No, I'm not,' he said.

'Well, you're on fire, then,' I said, ''cos there's smoke coming out of your coat! Can't you read that sign?'

Straight away the lad started kicking off, shouting and swearing and punching. I should have known better: I knew enough about dyslexia and other reading difficulties. He couldn't read and he thought I was taking the mickey out of him.

I did have to keep him off the bus that night, but once we were outside I apologized to him. I told him he was off the bus for smoking, but I wasn't going to bar him for having a go at me, because I'd been in the wrong, and I shouldn't have said what I said. We never had any trouble with him after that.

It's a good example of the kind of awareness we need. Some of our kids can't read or write, some come from difficult and violent home situations, and they bring all these sensitivities with them. It makes their behaviour very volatile, and we have to strike a balance: we need to understand them as individuals, but at the same time set firm boundaries for behaviour, so that the rules are the same for everyone. It's a way of making everyone feel secure.

Our volunteers are very special people, and many of them have their own amazing stories to tell. A good example is Kerry, who was introduced to me by one of my colleagues on the bus. He said that she wanted to help with the bus work, so we went along to meet her. She didn't need much prompting to share her testimony, and before long she was standing up in the God Slot and telling a crowd of young people, too. You could have heard a pin drop as she told her story.

Kerry had heard about God in lessons at school, and she asked her mum about him. 'Well, God's like a fairytale that some people believe in,' she said. 'A bit like Father Christmas.' Kerry thought that sounded a bit stupid, and decided she wasn't going to believe in God. She had a difficult home life, and grew up lacking in confidence. When Kerry was fifteen she suffered from severe depression and was admitted to a psychiatric hospital, where she was put on a complicated drug regime. What she didn't realize was that she could get addicted to some of these drugs, and before long she was resorting to all sorts of tricks to get more: lying to the nurses, stealing drugs or buying them from other patients.

When she was discharged she was sent to a Social Services hostel and managed to get a job, but she still needed to buy drugs. It wasn't easy to get hold of enough diazepam on the street, so she tried other things – cannabis at first, then heroin. She didn't like the hostel, but she wasn't earning enough to pay rent and buy drugs too, so she moved in with a drug dealer who lived in the same street. There she got into the terrible cycle of drug addiction: getting up in the morning and taking whizz or coke to get the energy to go out and score – and then buying more stuff to come back down.

Soon money became a real issue. At that time she scarcely realized the trouble she was getting into – her need for the drugs blotted everything else out. She transported drugs for the dealers she knew, and did some selling. She was mixing with some seriously hard guys, who found her innocent good looks useful. They would do burglaries and steal cash cards and chequebooks. Then they would get Kerry to fake signatures and spin the bank staff a story about having to get cash for her mum. They would make small withdrawals from a cash machine to check that an account was working OK, then send Kerry in to talk to the bank manager and explain that she needed to make a £6,000 withdrawal. She could hardly believe that they got away with it for so long, but she usually got the money. She handed it over and they would give her a small cut of the profits. Looking back, she described herself as naïve and desperate for money.

She was desperate for love, too, and she tried to find it by sleeping around, even prostitution, telling herself that if a man wanted to sleep with her it surely meant that he liked her – but realizing every time that it probably wasn't true. She was estranged from her family, and had no real friends – only people she did deals with. She ended up living rough on the streets.

One winter night she had climbed into the back of a smashed-up car to get out of the wind, but she was so cold that her body was numb. She felt lost and alone, and she knew she was literally freezing. She thought, 'This is the last time I'm going to feel anything.' She knew that if she went to sleep in those temperatures, she would die. She looked up at the sky and said, 'God, if you're out there, I've really messed up, and I'm sorry. I wish I could tell my family that I loved them. I know I could have done better and I know you probably won't want me, but this is it.' She said her prayer, closed her eyes and went to sleep, not expecting to wake up.

When she woke up the next morning she was surprised, but she didn't stop to think that God might have saved her. Life went on in the same way. She moved in with a boyfriend and got pregnant, and a couple of weeks later she got into a fight with a bus driver, and found herself running away from the police. Jumping on another bus to get away, she sat down next to a guy who seemed concerned about her.

'You look pretty freaked,' he said. 'Have you been smoking crack? I used to do drugs, but I'm a Christian now.'

'Oh, what a nutter!' she thought, but she liked the

feeling of someone taking an interest in her. A week or so later she bumped into another man from a church where she sometimes collected a food parcel. 'Here we go again,' she thought, as he started to tell her that Jesus loved her. Then one day she was watching her boyfriend playing basketball when a girl came and sat on the bench beside her. 'Why aren't you playing?' she asked.

'I'm pregnant,' Kerry replied. Usually at this point in the conversation the other person would say, 'When's the baby due?', but this girl said, 'Can I pray for you?'

'Oh, no,' Kerry thought, 'here's another one! My face must just attract you guys.' She had forgotten about her prayer, and it didn't occur to her until later that it was only after she had prayed for the first time that all these Christians kept popping up in her life.

Eventually she was persuaded to go on an Alpha course, and she enjoyed it. It made her happy to feel that someone was paying attention to her, but by now, she didn't really trust anyone because she had been used and let down so many times. She didn't know what a real friend was. She had split with her boyfriend, because once their son was born, Kerry wanted to sort her life out for his sake, but the boyfriend wasn't willing to give up his drugs. She met up with the Christians from time to time, and she really wanted to believe what they were telling her, that God cared for her and had better things in store for her. But somehow she couldn't bring herself to believe that anything in her life could change.

Then one day she was sitting in her kitchen while the baby was asleep. She recalls:

'I looked down and I could see this little ant crawling round on the floorboards. He was going round and round in circles, up and down, really busy, but he wasn't going anywhere. And I thought, "Well, I won't squash you, I'll put you out of the window."

'And I went and got a piece of paper and put it down in front of him, but he kept veering away. I was following him round with this piece of paper, trying to pick him up so he wouldn't get stomped on. I was talking to him and saying, "Look, the offer's in front of you – just climb on. I know I'm big and I know I'm scary and I know you don't know what I am, but just step on the paper and believe in me."

'And then he did – he crawled onto the paper, and I carried him over to the window and put him safely outside.

'And then I thought, "Hang on – that's what these Christians keep asking me to do, just step on and have faith in something I don't really understand."'

Kerry realized that she had tried to save herself and it hadn't worked. She'd tried every angle to make herself feel loved, and everything had ended in disaster. She thought, 'I really need to do this.' At that moment she knew that she believed, and that she had faith.

'As soon as I realized it, I felt as if a big weight had lifted off me. I was jumping around the room with excitement. I suddenly knew that I was worth something, I was special, and God cared about me enough to follow me round till I accepted him.'

As a child I wondered why I didn't have a mum and dad like other kids, and why no one in my family ever wanted to contact me.

Lee Abbey was the place where Gillian and I met, and where a good deal of my healing and growing took place.

Later I took groups of young people to the Beacon Youth Centre for their first experience of life outside Manchester.

The Robinson family: John, Gillian, Natalie and Leah

The Bus Ministry: Eden Bus 1: Rose Lancaster's birthday present!

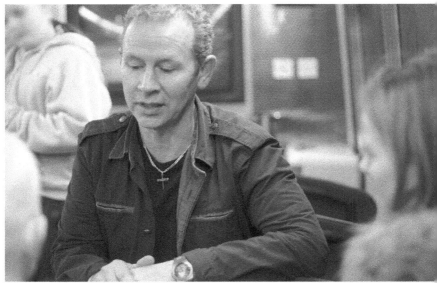

Every night on the bus is different, as young people come to have fun, meet their friends, and talk to the volunteers about the things that matter to them.

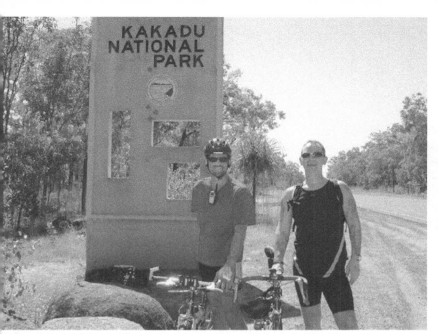

Paul and I rode 240km in blistering temperatures to raise funds for The Message.

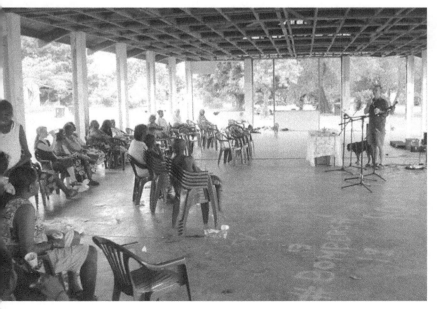

Speaking in a church with no walls, on the other side of the world – yet I felt very close to these people who live on the margins of society.

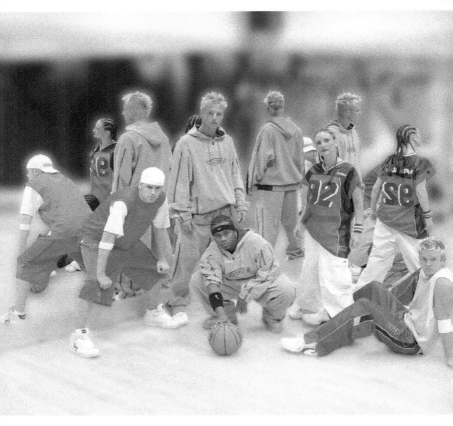

The Tribe reached young people by singing about God in language everyone could understand – with music they loved.

Manchester is a thriving city – yet it has run-down areas of high unemployment and high crime. The Eden Teams live and work in these communities.

David Cameron, the Conservative party leader, came to see the bus ministry for himself.

It was a huge surprise when I received the Unsung Hero award for our work on the bus ministry. Linda Robson, centre, was a true star and read out some of my story.

Kerry had a hard struggle after that, because she had learned all the habits of being rejected and thinking she was worthless, but gradually she got stronger. 'I realized I didn't have to go to extreme lengths to be loved – I could just be me.'

These days she has a new confidence – confidence enough to stand up on the bus and tell her story. All her rage and bitterness has gone, and in its place she finds she has love in her heart, which she wants to share. 'I want people to feel the happiness I feel – specially that moment when I realized I was worth more, and I jumped around my kitchen with joy! I've learned to love myself, and I've learned to love and respect other people, too.'

Kerry is just one of our bus helpers, an ordinary single mum living on a tough estate. But she is a wonderful person, and hers is an amazing story of how a life can be changed by an amazing God.

Chapter 6

UNLOCKING THE DOOR

As I worked on the bus and got to know the various areas of Manchester better and better, I was also getting to know more about the work that The Message was doing. Over the years the projects evolved and changed – not just the bands and the Eden Projects, but other ideas which were developed to meet specific needs. There's Life Centre, a youth café where young people can find a whole range of things, from training and IT resources to counselling services and sports and leisure activities. The Big Deal is a wide-ranging community project which sets up small events in different areas – like The Big Bike Ride, The Big Teacup and so on. It contacts different organizations such as the police, the local council and the churches, and gets them working together and cooperating. The small one-off events usually generate much more long-lasting relationships and ongoing work. Genetik is another initiative that offers opportunities for people to get involved with its music ministry, evangelism and discipleship training. All these projects came out of The Message Trust's concern for reaching every young person in Manchester, meeting their needs and talking to them about God in language they could understand.

I was specially interested in Reflex, the prison work that was being rolled out across Young Offender Institutions across the north-west. The idea was to put a team into each institution, working in partnership with other Christian agencies. The volunteers would befriend the young offenders while they were still inside, and be ready to offer them help when they were released, finding them work and places to live and linking them with local churches and Eden Project teams. I knew how badly that was needed.

I was fourteen when I was locked up for the first time, sentenced to six weeks in a detention centre for arson. It was a terrible shock: I honestly believed the fire was an accident. I'll never forget that sound of doors being slammed and keys being turned in the lock. During the day we were kept busy cooking in the kitchen, washing floors and cleaning the toilets. The days were hard, but the nights were terrible. We slept in dormitories, and the bully boys would come and roll you up in a blanket and give you a beating. If you made any noise they used to put a sock in your mouth and tie it there. The staff must have known what was happening, but they didn't do anything. I think the place was easier to run if there was a pecking order established among the boys.

When I was seventeen I was arrested for burglary, and spent five weeks in the local remand centre. It was another grim place, filled with young men who lived violent lives, and there were plenty of fights and beatings. That was where I was so depressed that I tried to commit suicide. I couldn't see any way of breaking out of a hopeless life. I couldn't break away from the gang I hung out with, because I had no job, no home and no money. I thought, 'This is all there is to life: running with a gang of people I'm afraid of, or getting locked up in a prison cell. I've got no future and no hope.' I stole an aluminium ashtray from the staffroom when I was cleaning it, and that night in my cell I bent the metal until it tore in two. Then I used the jagged edges to slit my wrists. The result was that I made my life even worse than it had been: my injuries were stitched up in the prison medical unit, then I was put in a straitjacket and placed in a solitary cell.

Eventually my case came to court and I was sentenced to eighteen months in borstal – the forerunner of today's Young Offender Institutions. Once again there was a strict regime of work and fitness training, but this time I was put into a single cell. It had a bed, a sink and a toilet, and I suppose the good thing was that no one could get in to beat you up at night – though by then I had learned to handle myself, and I could (and did) fight with the toughest. Those nights were long and lonely, though, and I had plenty of time to think. I promised myself that I would never do anything to get banged up in prison ever again. How could I have been so stupid? Yet when I was released, I didn't have the first idea of how to make a decent life for myself. I bumped into a few of my old mates, went for a drink with them, and slipped back into the same old ways.

Part of the problem was the lack of support. I'd had no real experience of life, and I didn't know how to apply for a job or even how to go about finding help with housing. I'd been offered a place in a hostel, but it sounded too much like the prison I'd just left, and anyway I didn't know anyone there. At least back on the streets I had my old mates, a few familiar faces. I couldn't get a job: no one would take me on when they knew I was homeless and had been in borstal. It was a vicious circle: no money meant I couldn't find a place to live. No home meant I couldn't give an address to an employer, so I couldn't get a job. No job meant no money...and so it went round. It wasn't until I met Tony and his wife Sylvia – the wonderful Christian couple who took me in, let me share their home and gave me work to do – that I was able, for the first time, to learn how to live a normal life. Having work and earning some money gave me some self-esteem, something else that I lacked.

I knew from first-hand experience what kind of life led young people into prison in the first place; I knew how terrible prison life could be for them; and I knew how badly they needed support if they were ever going to stay out of prison and make a new start. The Reflex project is a brilliant idea, and it was triggered by the realization that if the mission of The Message is to reach all the young people in Greater Manchester, then surely the young people in Young Offender Institutions are among the most needy and hopeless of all. Suicide rates in these prisons are at a record level, such is the despair felt by those young inmates. Their one hope and chance of breaking free from the destructive lives they are living is the freedom and purpose that only Jesus can bring. If we can reach them with that message of hope, and back it up by the practical love and help they need, then there is a great work to be done for God.

I had thought for a long time that my experience of prison meant that one day God would want me to work for him there. In fact, I had already had one brush with employment in the prison system, which hadn't worked out too well. When Gillian and I were first thinking about moving on from Southampton, I saw a job advertised for an assistant chaplain in a Young Offender Institution in Market Drayton, and I applied and was interviewed. The interview went well, and as I left I heard the chaplain say, 'Yes! He's just what we're looking for!' It was a great boost to my self-confidence when I received the formal offer of a job, but only a few days later I had a phone call from the prison governor, saying that he didn't want me after all. I couldn't understand it, as everyone there had known all about my previous convictions and everything about me – I had been completely honest and hadn't held anything back. I was offended that the post could be snatched away from me after I'd been offered it on my own merits, because I was the best man for the job.

I wrote to Jack Straw (then Home Secretary) saying how wrong it was to interview someone and offer a job, and then retract the offer. By then I was deeply confused: was this job part of God's will for us or not? I prayed about it and came to the conclusion that God's answer was 'Not yet' for prison work. Two weeks later I got another letter reinstating the original job offer, but by then I had already accepted my job with The Message. All the same, I praised God and thanked him for the experience, because the whole thing had been good for me. It had showed me that I was good enough for that work, and that I could be valued for who I was and because of the experiences of my past life, not just in spite of them.

So when I started looking closely at the possibility of working with the Reflex project, I thought that perhaps this was to be my way into prison work. Maybe now the time was right. The job as Prison Team Leader looked interesting: after a couple of years of working on the Bus Ministry, I knew several young people currently in local Young Offender Institutions, some of them the elder brothers of kids who came regularly to the buses. It would be good to be part of the team that offered help and hope to them. All the same, it would be hard to give up the Bus Ministry, which I loved, and who would take over from me?

As so often happens, the right man came along at just the right time. Steve had moved up from the south of England, like us, and he was a gifted youth worker. As soon as I met him I knew he would be able to handle all the complex aspects of the Bus Ministry, so I felt more than happy to hand over to him. In fact, he had plenty of work to do: we'd had several attacks on the buses, and one night there was a serious fire on Eden Bus 2. Miraculously, that night the bus hadn't been parked under cover, where it usually was, but in the yard. This not only saved the shed from burning down, but also meant that Eden Bus 1 wasn't harmed. Even so, there was a lot of repair work to be planned, paid for and coordinated, and it kept Steve pretty busy for a while.

Meanwhile, I became part of the chaplaincy team in the four Young Offender Institutions in and around Greater Manchester. I knew it was a privilege, and I believed that it was God's will for me, yet I can't describe my feelings when I made my first visit, and I heard that characteristic sound of the doors slamming behind me, and the jingle of the keys on the prison officer's chain as he unlocked and locked every door we went through. You might have heard that sound on television programmes, even in comedies like Ronnie Barker's *Porridge*, but it doesn't convey the dread that you feel when it happens for real.

Real prisons aren't filled with cheeky lovable rogues like Norman Stanley Fletcher, engaged in humorous banter and mischievous battles of wits with comic prison officers. They're filled with desperate, hurting, rejected people, who long to be free, but who, through circumstances and their own bad choices, are stuck in a cycle of destruction. I knew it because I had once been one of them. As soon as the first door slammed behind me I felt as if I'd made a leap back in time through twenty years to my youth – to being shut in to serve a sentence that seemed to go on for ever. I followed the prison officer through the corridors to the landing where I was going to work, trying to look cool, calm and collected, but in fact I was sweating and shaking.

When *Nobody's Child* was published, lots of people read the book, and I started getting even more invitations to speak in prisons as well as in churches and at Christian events. So I'd visited prisons and Young Offender Institutions lots of times, and every time I'd found those first few minutes scary, but those were only flying visits. I knew I would go in, meet the chaplain, go down to the chapel or the gym where I was speaking, deliver my talk, maybe chat to a few prisoners, and then I'd be out again, all within a couple of hours. This time it was different. This was going to be my working environment: I was going to have to come here every day, and go through the door-slamming and key-jangling over and over again. I wondered how long it would take for me to get used to it.

One of the hardest things was being locked on a landing for a whole evening, knowing that I couldn't just turn and walk away when I wanted. For those few hours, I was as much a prisoner as the young men I was talking to, and even though I was there voluntarily, I still found it nerve-racking. I got over my initial feelings of panic, but I still had to deal with being back 'inside'.

Every time I think I've arrived at a stable place where the past can't hurt me any more, I get into some situation like this and find that I'm not as strong as I thought I was. Sometimes it's surroundings like these that bring back memories I'd rather not have – I want to lock them away and forget them. Sometimes it's the young people talking about their lives – being let down and rejected, feeling like scum because they've allowed themselves to be sucked into crime or drink or drugs. I know what that feels like, and it brings back all the times when I felt completely worthless. It stirs up feelings inside me, and I know that I haven't left them behind completely yet.

I believe that God is still dealing with the damage

in my life and is still in the process of healing me. I think of it like a bottle of fizzy lemonade: if you take the top off all at once, it fizzes up and spills over and makes a terrible mess. If I had to face up to all the hurt and rejection and pain and anger at once, I couldn't cope. Instead, he's letting in the air little by little, letting the pressure off and calming the turmoil that's hidden inside. It's a gradual healing, and though perhaps I'd like it all to be over and done with, I know that his way is thorough and, in the end, it is the best.

It's like thinking about being in God's presence. We couldn't handle being exposed to his holiness and purity, so he gives us little tastes and glimpses of himself, to prepare us and help us to understand him more and more as time goes by. I trust in his healing, and I believe it will one day be complete in all of us. There have been many times when I've walked away from a prison after listening to some young guys telling me their stories, and I have cried to God and asked him to work in their lives the way he has in mine.

Sometimes I've been talking to the toughest young people, who have already been through so much pain and trouble in their lives, and I've said, 'Do you know that God cares about you? If not, I can tell you I'm a hundred and ten per cent sure that he loves you and wants your life to be so much different. And I know that because of what God has done in my life.' Lots of them say, 'I can so relate to your story!' Lots of them grew up in care, too, and they've all fallen into crime for one reason or another. They look at my tattoos and my scars, and they start asking how God changed my life.

I've learned something really important – that all those terrible experiences weren't just a horrible mistake. Those memories are not a meaningless part of my life that I should reject and lock away and throw away the key – even though I'd like to, because it's so painful to recall those dark times. I believe the devil tried to destroy me in the past, through rejection, through loneliness, through violence and danger. But God wants to use me. He takes the things that the devil tried to destroy me with, and he turns them into tools that he can use. The pain and destruction of my past make the bridge between me and young people in similar circumstances, so I can relate to them and do his work of reaching out to them. I can stand up covered in tattoos and scars and say, 'Look what God has done in my life.' My past can be used for God.

When I spent an evening on the landings, I was usually just talking to the lads. Some of them were on remand, waiting for their case to come to court, so they knew that soon they would either be sentenced or released. It made them nervous and edgy, especially as the court date approached. Even when they were pretty sure they'd get a custodial sentence, they were always tormented by a shred of hope that they might get a community sentence and be released. The lads who had already been sentenced were a bit more laid back: they knew how long they'd got to serve, and they generally had a lot of time on their hands. They liked to sit down and talk to me about their lives. None of them wanted to come back to prison, ever, but many of them had a shrewd idea of how hard it might be to make a new start when they got out. One or two of them had read *Nobody's Child*, and they looked at me and said, 'Well, if you can do it, I can do it.' It was very encouraging.

Mostly, I just chatted to them the way I talk to the kids on the buses, listening to what they have to say, and offering a bit about my own life and the difference that Jesus has made to me whenever it's appropriate. There were usually one or two prison officers around, and often they were listening in, too. I tried to feel at home in the prison environment, but I still got things wrong sometimes. One night I was told off by a prison officer for going into a cell and not 'double-locking' the door first, so that it couldn't be locked from the inside. He was angry because I could have been taken hostage – I'd put myself and others at risk – and I should have known better. I was still on a learning curve.

We ran a Youth Alpha course in the prison chapel, and that brought about some amazing conversations. One evening I was sitting next to a young man when we showed the DVD of *Nobody's Child*, and I could tell that something was stirring in him. When we stood up at the end he turned to me and said, 'Will you pray for me, John?' Then he put his hands on my shoulders and bent his head forward until our foreheads were touching. It looked a bit weird and people must have wondered what we were doing, but there was a sense of real contact. We prayed together and he asked Christ to come into his life and change it. It was such a privilege to share that moment with him.

Another evening a guy said to me, 'It's a great story, John, an amazing story, and you've done well for yourself. But I don't believe in what you believe in.'

I said to him, 'So what's your story, then, mate? 'Cos I can tell you're very angry and bitter about what's happened to you.'

'Yeah, I am,' he said. 'I came home from school one day and there was a note on the kitchen table from my mum and dad. They'd gone to Spain to live, and they said they wouldn't be coming back.'

He'd been left to fend for himself at the age of sixteen, and he was still filled with anger and resentment, and the feeling that he mattered so little to his own mum and dad that they just went off and left him. I said to him, 'Listen, whatever your parents think, God thinks you're amazing. He thinks you're a prince. And he never leaves, and he never walks out on you. People may let you down, but God never will.'

We saw some amazing changes in the young people we worked with in those institutions. I loved building them up and saying, 'God can use you like he's using me. You're so valuable and precious in his eyes.' I know the devil doesn't like that. He wants to see these young lives destroyed, and that's part of his plan. But God's plan is to save and rescue them and build them up, to his glory. He can give us back our past – 'I will repay you for the years the locusts have eaten' (Joel 2:25) – and he can give us a future too.

I had a great time as Prison Team Leader, and I loved to share my testimony, talk and take part in services, but after a while I realized that something was missing. I enjoyed working in the Young Offender

Institutions, but I was even more excited about work-ing with the young people when they got out of prison, when they were back on the streets and facing all the temptations of their former lives. The institu-tions were closed communities, not the real outside world, and that was where I wanted to be and to work with them. I hesitated for a long time, but eventually I decided to talk to Andy Hawthorne about how I was feeling. To my surprise he told me that Steve (my replacement as leader of the Bus Ministry) and his wife wanted to move back to the south of England, and that they had been praying about their next move. Steve had got another job almost immediately and everything had fallen into place for them. Andy was pleased for them – but it meant that the buses were standing idle.

As soon as I heard that, I knew that I wanted my old job back. I had longed to support the prison min-istry, but this wasn't my work. God had taught me another lesson: you can weigh everything up in terms of experience and suitability, and you can go off and do what you think you should be doing, but it may not be God's plan. Just as before, I had to accept that, even though I seemed to be admirably qualified for and suited to the work in human terms, it wasn't what God wanted me to do.

Maybe God will want me to work in prisons one day in the future. Maybe the timing wasn't right. Or maybe I just needed to learn that lesson – that noth-ing is wasted, and that there is no experience, how-ever bad, that God can't take and use and turn into something beautiful for him. I still go into prisons to speak at special events, and of course I visit if young people ask me to, but it's not my main vision. Right now, the Bus Ministry is what I do, and I love being out on the street, working with young people and meeting them in their own area and their everyday lives. If I have any gifts in youth work – my ability to reach young people and understand their lives and talk to them honestly about the love of God – they come out of the damage of my past. My past is part of who I am.

Chapter 7   # THE VICAR'S WIFE

By this time Gillian's work in our church was building up, and her faithful adherence to her vision was bearing fruit. She was always seeking to work on the renewal of faith within the church, combined with providing opportunities for those outside it to find faith. We both see so many damaged people outside the church, and we know that God can help them. That's why reaching people with the good news of Jesus has always been our passion.

We ran Alpha courses where people came to find God, and they built up the faith of the church family too. Recently we had a confirmation service for twelve adults, and the Bishop asked Gillian to provide a short history for each person. As she wrote those stories down, she was struck by what an amazing couple of pages they made. Several people had suffered abuse as children that had affected them as adults, and they had found freedom in Jesus for the first time in their lives. One woman said, 'Well, if I'd known that the Holy Spirit could heal me, I wouldn't have bothered with all those years of counselling!'

As we talked about it, we realized that it's easy – especially when your work is so closely linked with your faith – to get caught up in the routine and mundane parts of church life. It's good sometimes to reflect on what God is doing in people's lives. It's only when we look back on the road we have all travelled together as a church, that we see how far God has brought us. Nowadays we have a congregation of around seventy or eighty at the main service, plus about fifty children, and all age groups are represented.

It's great for me, because although the church is Gillian's field of mission and work, it's also my resting place, the place where I go to be fed, to share in fellowship with the church family, and to build up my own Christian life so that I have something to offer when I go out to do my work on the buses.

Part of Gillian's job includes being a governor of the church primary school in the parish, and as the vicar she also takes assemblies every week. It's a fantastic mission field. The children's response to her assemblies was so good that some of them said they'd like to come to Sunday School – but their parents didn't want to go to church and wouldn't bring them. So Gillian decided to take the Sunday School to the children, and started running a school club at lunchtime once a week. It's called FPW, or Funky Prayer Warriors (the children chose the name!), and around forty children attend. In fact, it's so popular that she's now struggling with the numbers – there isn't room to accommodate the next class coming up from the infants to the juniors, so she now needs to start another lunchtime session for these extra twenty children. There is one little boy with a sad little face who regularly pleads to be allowed to come to the club, but there simply hasn't been space.

Ours is an ordinary area, and some of these are tough kids, but they are lively and interested and they just absorb God. It's great that kids who aren't taken to church by their parents have responded so well to the opportunity to meet God and get to know his love. In one assembly Gillian asked, 'How do you know God is real?' A tough little lad of about ten put his hand up and answered, 'Because I can hear him in my heart.' I thought it was amazing that he was willing to say that in front of all his friends.

Another day Gillian showed the DVD of *Nobody's Child* to a class of eleven-year-olds, who were preparing to go up to secondary school. At the end, she noticed that one lad had tears in his eyes. He'd obviously identified with some of what he'd seen. In front of the whole class he put his hand up and said, 'I was going to run away before I saw that today, but I'm not going to do it now.'

It's an example of the way that sometimes our ministries overlap, and I get involved in what Gillian is doing. She was concerned for the young people in our own area, but the Bus Ministry can't get everywhere, so we sat down to think what we could provide for them. In the end we came up with an idea we'd tried successfully before, in Southampton – a non-alcoholic bar. That first bar is still doing well, with around 100 young people visiting it regularly, so we knew it could be done.

We identified a suitable space – a room just off the main church which was being used as a combined vestry and storage area. It doesn't bother me when I see parts of church buildings being used as cafés or shops – to me, a building is just a building. It's the people of God, filled with the Holy Spirit, who make it a church. This room was pretty untidy, full of old boxes and things, and it needed clearing out and redecorating, but we realized that between us we'd got the skills to do it fairly cheaply. Gillian and the girls cleared out the massive spiders; Sarah Green, one of our church family, worked out a wacky colour scheme and a group of them helped me do the painting and decorating; Andy Clements, who also works with me on the Bus Ministry, did the electrics, and Paul Cooper (our churchwarden) built the rest from scratch! I designed the bar and we installed a kitchen area and seating. We managed to get about £2,000 in grants from the Youth Parish Mission Fund, and that paid for some of the setting-up. We made it look just like an ordinary bar – we even have a big screen on one wall – and the only difference is that we serve 'Amethyst' non-alcoholic cocktails. The syrups are supplied by a specialist Christian company.

We're open every Saturday from 7.30 to 9.00 p.m., and we have at least two adults on duty. Alice was involved from the start, before God called her to Canada, and since then we have been joined by John and Sarah who have been a real blessing to the bar and, most importantly, to the young people. We make sure that the church is warm and lit, and we have another adult from the congregation on duty in there, because the young people have to walk through the church to reach the bar. When they open the door and see the bar for the first time, they're amazed! Usually we get around thirty people per night, but one evening recently we had over fifty, and they spilled out into the church and sat down there to chat. The people in the church kept telling them to go through into the bar, but they couldn't because there wasn't enough room!

Most of the young people who come have no Christian faith and they don't come to church. They just enjoy coming to the bar, chilling out with their friends. We don't have any specific activities, except for the occasional Quiz Night, just like you'd get in a pub. However, every week just before we close up, I run the equivalent of the God Slot – the kids call it John's Corner or John's Talk Time. I share my testimony or a story from the Bible, and we take prayer requests. There's no pressure on anyone to stay, but we never have anyone leaving early or missing it.

Another innovation in our church is something called Taste and See. It's a monthly event for local people, where we taste food from all over the world (or even a ham sandwich!) and have a speaker. They may share their testimony or talk about their work – for instance, we've had a couple talking about their work with abandoned children in China. We have the food part of the meeting in a lounge room, but we move through into the church to hear the speaker, because we aren't ashamed of being Christians and we want people to get used to being in church in a relaxed and unthreatening atmosphere.

I was the speaker on one occasion, and I was more nervous that night than I've ever been. It's one thing to share your testimony with a hall full of strangers, but it's something else to stand up and talk about yourself in front of the neighbours! I was quite happy when I looked out and saw that not many people were there, but when the church started filling up I got quite anxious. That week a woman came to church for the first time and told Gillian that she was there 'because of your husband's talk'. She had suffered a lot of rejection, and wanted to know how she could be free of it, because she knew it was damaging her life. Gillian explained to her that God can set us free, and she became a Christian that night.

We had one teenager who came to the bar regularly, and she brought her mum and dad along to a Taste and See session. It was wonderful to see the whole family there together, and to see her so excited about bringing them. She has trained as the bar manager, and she's growing in confidence all the time. She's soon going to be confirmed, and now her dad has started coming to church with her.

I enjoy my Saturday evenings, though it's bit of a busman's holiday for me – literally! I have a nice night off from working with young people on the Bus Ministry, and I spend it working with young people in the bar. Apart from the bar, I try not to get involved too much with the rest of the youth work in the church, because then I'd never get a break. For a long time I was involved with our Sunday morning young people's group, but I knew that I had to take time to be fed by God instead of giving out all the time. Still, I feel I should do something for the young people in my own church, as well as for those in the Greater Manchester area which is The Message's mission field. I have a commitment and a responsibility to help our own church family.

During the week I do my job – the administrative work for the bus, training new volunteers in everything from child protection legislation to anger management and youth work skills, visiting schools or prisons, and going out on the bus on some evenings. Meanwhile, Gillian is kept busy doing hers – church meetings, pastoral visiting, mentoring, counselling, preparing sermons and planning worship, and helping in the church school. Sometimes it can be a fight to fit everything in, especially when you live in a vicarage, which always seems to be open house. Gillian officially works part-time, but her hours can be very long, because you can't turn people away if they come to you in a crisis. There are so many needy, hurting people whose lives are in a mess; often they have never known any hope, and they need love and they need God. We have encouraged our church to become a place where everyone can find hope in Jesus.

One of the practical problems is that diocesan structures don't really cater for growing churches: staff are allocated according to the size of the parish, not according to how many people are actually coming to the church, or what kind of work is going on there. Other churches may be full of people who like to come to a service on a Sunday and maybe attend a mid-week group, but that's all. By contrast, our church is full of new Christians who have been so overcome by the power of God that they want to give their all. They want to live their lives for God, and that's absolutely wonderful – but it can mean a lot of work to channel their energy and enthusiasm. Add to that the number of personal problems that arise in any area where there's a certain amount of poverty and a fair few social issues, and there's always a lot going on. That not only adds to Gillian's workload, it also affects me and the girls. We have to work hard to find time to be a family.

There can sometimes be tensions if I have to work a weekend, or certain nights in the week, when Gillian has something in her diary, too. Most of her parish meetings are held in the evenings, and if it's a night when I'm working, they have to happen in the vicarage so she can be at home with Natalie and Leah. We have to think of them, too: we don't want our children to grow up thinking that mum and dad were so busy doing God's work that they had no time for them. The girls understand that we work hard because we want to help people and tell them about God, but we don't want them to grow up resenting it, so we have had to learn to schedule time as a family. The best times are when we go off for a bike ride together, or just have fun chatting about what they've been up to at school or playing with their friends. We have given our lives to serve God, but our children need our attention, too.

When Leah was seven or eight she started having problems at school. At first her teachers thought she might have a hearing problem, because her spelling was so unusual: even now she will write 'Richard' as 'frigud' for example. Tests confirmed that her hearing was OK, but that was just the start of a long and painful series of tests and assessments. Eventually she was diagnosed not just with dyslexia – problems with reading, writing and sequencing – but also with dyspraxia. This condition, which causes coordination difficulties (Leah has muscle weakness and a slight tremor in her left hand), has been called the 'hidden handicap'. It can cause severe social and educational problems for the child. Any parent who has had a child with special needs will know how difficult this can be within the school environment. Eventually we moved the girls to our church school, where the special educational needs support has been much better.

The diagnosis gives Leah a special link with me, because my own dyslexia wasn't identified until I was an adult. She knows that I understand her problems, and she can also see that I have come through and manage to run my life, even though reading and writing aren't my favourite activities. It hurts me when I see the social rejection which she suffers: other children sometimes leave her out of games because of her clumsiness, and she finds certain social situations difficult. I want so much to protect her, because I know what it feels like to stand on the edge of things, looking on. However, she has a firm faith, which is a tremendous joy for us. She makes up her own worship songs and they are always songs of praise: she is a little girl who has learned to trust God through her difficulties.

At night we always have a story, a chat and a prayer time with the girls separately, and Leah often needs extra time to talk about her day, because that's when she processes her difficulties and works out ways of dealing with things. But we have two children, and it has been hard for Natalie because Leah has needed so much attention. We realized this when Natalie said one night, 'If I tell you some stories about school, will you stay longer with me, too?' They teach us, and we learn.

Natalie is very quick-witted, and shares my wacky sense of humour. One day recently Leah and Gillian went out to do some shopping, but Natalie didn't want to go. 'Dad and me are going to do the housework, and he's promised we can put loud music on and be silly!' She was really excited at the prospect!

I find all this fascinating, because I never knew my parents, so I didn't know what to expect from my relationship with my own children. The girls say that I'm a softy, and they know they can wrap me round their little fingers. Gillian tends to be the disciplinarian in our house, because the girls know I can't bear to be hard on them. She imposes the same loving discipline that she had as a child, such as 'No pudding if you don't finish your dinner.' Natalie knows she only has to pull a silly sad face, and I'll melt and give in.

Working with young people as I do, I see children younger than my own who already have major problems. It makes me all the more determined to nurture my own family, and to enjoy the girls while they're young. I'm so proud of them, and I want to enjoy being their dad.

On Saturdays, if I'm not working, we make time as a family for shopping, outings or even (excitingly) housework! In the evening Gillian may share her sermon with me, so on Sunday I get a rerun – but I still have to try to look interested and enthusiastic about it. (I don't always manage it, and sometimes she catches me yawning.) I like to just sit there in the pew and take it all in, and pretend to myself that I haven't heard it all before, because it's my chance to learn and grow. I enjoy going to church and not being in charge, just being me – worshipping, taking in God's word and meeting up with the church family.

People laugh when I say that on Sundays I have to be the vicar's wife, but that's essentially what it is. It's my job to support Gillian, and I can do that in lots of ways. After the service she'll be chatting to people at the door, and I do my bit, sometimes talking to the young people, sometimes to the men, because some of them may find it difficult to relate to a female vicar. People often compare Gillian to Dawn French as the Vicar of Dibley because they both laugh a lot!

Quite often the girls will come up with some plan they've hatched with the other children, and say, 'Louise's mum says we can go and play at her house', because they've worked out that if Mum and Dad are both busy, we're more likely to agree. Later we realize we've been manoeuvred into plans we didn't quite understand at the time or weren't concentrating on!

Then we go home and have lunch, and after lunch it's time for family games – we all love board-games like Boggle, Monopoly, Battleships or The Game of Life. I love this relaxed family time, when we're all laughing and teasing each other and playing together. Gillian and I have always bounced ideas and jokes off each other, and the girls are picking up on that and joining in. Our house is a lovely, lively house, full of fun and laughter.

It's not all plain sailing. Ours is just a normal marriage – you don't get any short cuts just because she's a vicar – and we still have a few barneys. If we've had an argument on a Saturday night (yes, I know you're not supposed to let the sun go down on your anger, but we're only human and these things happen), it's all the harder to sit in church the next morning and listen to my wife preaching. I sit there in the pew with a face like I'm chewing a wasp, thinking, 'I'm not listening! I don't want to know!' I know it's childish, but it's hard to see her standing up there in a position of authority when we haven't resolved our differences. But somewhere about halfway through, it always comes home to me that Gillian is preaching the word of God, and that's what I'm listening to. (And she's not scoring any points off me.)

Occasionally being the 'vicar's wife' makes me want to do something outrageous – dance or light up a cigar or walk through the church with my pants on my head – anything wacky to ditch the image and prove that I'm just an ordinary person. (On second thoughts, maybe that last one wouldn't be very ordinary.) The problem is that there's a lot of pressure on clergy couples. There's an expectation that we'll always be there for people, offering counsel and support, and on one level that's exactly what we do, and it's a privilege to do it. But on another level we sometimes feel that when we have our own problems – like with Leah – it's difficult for us to find the support we need.

There are no days off when you live in a vicarage, and sometimes it feels as though we're living in a goldfish bowl – we're always under scrutiny. The doorbell is always ringing. Sometimes, on a hot summer day, I answer the door in a T-shirt, with all the tattoos and scars on show. If it's someone who doesn't know us, they generally say, 'Are *you* the vicar?' in disbelief, as if anyone looking like me couldn't possibly be.

'No, my wife is,' I reply.

'Your *wife* is?' they say, though whether they can't believe the vicar is a woman or they can't believe she's married to me, we never know.

Sometimes I'm tempted to sing, 'Yes, can I help you?' as if I'm singing the responses in a church, or to offer them a cucumber sandwich with the crusts cut off, just to debunk the whole 'life in the vicarage' image. Other times we say, 'Let's take the girls *out* for tea,' just to get away from the doorbell and the phone. It's not that we don't love our life, but occasionally we have to make space for us.

In fact, life's tricky enough just learning how to be a family. Gillian comes from a loving family, but I don't have any happy childhood memories to draw on. I only have bad memories of my foster homes, and though I was happy at Barnardo's, it wasn't a family environment, it was an institution, and the people who looked after us were professional staff. As a result, I always feel as if I might be getting things wrong. When Leah was born, I sent Gillian a Mother's Day card from me, because she was now a mother, and I didn't know that it was meant to come from the children. Christmas and birthdays are quite emotional times for me, because I didn't have many that were good when I was growing up. It was a part of the life that other people had, but was closed off to me. For a long time I didn't understand how it all worked: what did you have to do to make a fuss of someone on their birthday? What makes a family Christmas?

I still have little habits that hang on from the old days. It's a joke between me and Gillian that whenever I have new clothes, I keep wearing them: I take them off, put them through the wash and put them straight back on again. Gillian has nearly had to force me to change outfits, because as she says, other people won't know I've washed the clothes and put them back on! It's because I was never used to having a choice about what to put on: what I had was what I stood up in. I'm still a bit like a squirrel, collecting things and putting them away in a box or a bag. I've done a few counselling courses, and nowadays I understand that this sort of behaviour is typical of children who have been deprived – either materially (in terms of having no personal possessions) or emotionally (in terms of being starved of love). They hide things away because they are precious, and they think they will be taken away if they aren't guarded or hidden.

I also have a problem with packing for holidays or trips – I find it impossible to decide what to take with me. I've done ten charity bike rides in different places around the world, and when I arrive people always say, 'Where's the support team?' I reply, 'There's no team, just me.' And they say, 'So why have you got five suitcases?' It's because I've got five jumpers and twenty pairs of underpants and socks, even if I'm only away for a week. And in any case, when you're biking, you don't need an extensive and varied wardrobe – just your shorts and shirt, and you wash them and put them back on the next day. When we go away for the weekend as a family, Gillian laughs at me for insisting on taking every pair of shoes I own – even sandals, 'just in case', in the middle of winter! It's just that having enough clothes represents security for me.

I get a lot of support and understanding from Gillian and her family, and they've helped me to learn what family life is like. They've accepted me and made me feel a part of the family, and I'll always be grateful for that. Gillian's mum never takes sides – if Gillian rings her for a grumble or if we've had a row, she'll always ring and speak to me, too, so I won't feel as if I'm being excluded. Gillian's dad has been good, too, showing me how to do DIY jobs around the house, as a dad would do for a son of his own. Gillian's two sisters have become like sisters to me, and their families are part of my family, too.

Gillian and I try to work as a team, sharing the family responsibilities because we both have to juggle home and work in the same way. Even though Gillian is the vicar, leadership in the church is partly a joint effort. Sometimes I wish she could see me at work out on the bus in the evening, the way I'm able to see her when she's leading worship. It's not just that I'd like her to be proud of me, but I'd like her to see me doing what God has called me to do. She would love to come out on the bus with me, but we don't have babysitters for the children, so she prays for me at home. I'm proud of her, because I see that she's doing a good job, but I also see the Holy Spirit at work in her and through her. When she preaches she challenges and moves people, and the worship is amazing when you can feel that spiritual uplift when everyone is praising God wholeheartedly. We can share in that because we're there together.

Gillian rarely sees me at work, but sometimes I get that same feeling of being led by the Holy Spirit – that prompting of when to speak and when to be silent and listen; which kid needs attention; knowing the way to disarm the cocky and aggressive lads without putting them down or belittling them or robbing them of their fragile self-esteem. And we have our special moments, too, when someone who has never been interested in the God Slot comes upstairs and asks for prayer. I sometimes wish Gillian could be there to share those special moments. I often ring and ask her to pray during the evening, especially if something is kicking off. It's good to know that she's praying for my safety on the bus, and when I get home we really value being able to share together about our day. Church leadership can also be lonely, and we find it helpful to be able to offload to each other and pray together before we fall into bed at about midnight.

In 2006 we had a special treat, though – we were both invited to speak at Lee Abbey. It was great because that was where we met, so we had lots of happy memories of the place. It was a good moment to give thanks that God has blessed us with each other, and to realize how much we really do appreciate each other. We enjoyed working as a team. It was a long time since we'd been able to minister together outside of our home church, and it was good for me not to be the vicar's wife for once!